SWITZERLAND ON ALL FOURS

Trafford
PUBLISHING

Switzerland on All Fours

by

Lloyd P. Clark

Order this book online at www.trafford.com/08-0628
or email orders@trafford.com

Most Trafford titles are also available at major online book retailers.

Note for Librarians: A cataloguing record for this book is available from Library and Archives Canada at www.collectionscanada.ca/amicus/index-e.html

ISBN: 978-1-4251-7865-9

We at Trafford believe that it is the responsibility of us all, as both individuals and corporations, to make choices that are environmentally and socially sound. You, in turn, are supporting this responsible conduct each time you purchase a Trafford book, or make use of our publishing services. To find out how you are helping, please visit www.trafford.com/responsiblepublishing.html

Our mission is to efficiently provide the world's finest, most comprehensive book publishing service, enabling every author to experience success. To find out how to publish your book, your way, and have it available worldwide, visit us online at www.trafford.com/10510

Trafford
PUBLISHING   www.trafford.com

North America & international
toll-free: 1 888 232 4444 (USA & Canada)
phone: 250 383 6864 ♦ fax: 250 383 6804 ♦ email: info@trafford.com

The United Kingdom & Europe
phone: +44 (0)1865 722 113 ♦ local rate: 0845 230 9601
facsimile: +44 (0)1865 722 868 ♦ email: info.uk@trafford.com

10 9 8 7 6 5 4 3 2

Contents

Preface

T HE SWISS Alpine Pass Route makes use of a number of different paths both old and new to complete a traverse of the Swiss Alps between the medieval town of Sargans in the east and Montreux on the sun drenched shore of Lake Geneva in the west.

Weather conditions in Switzerland can be extremely changeable and should always be fully considered prior to attempting any walks across or among the Alps. We were extremely lucky for much of the walk but, with hindsight and maybe armed with better weather forecasts, the crossing of the Foo Pass would never have been attempted in the heavy June snows. In fact, had time been available, it would have been prudent to delay the start. That said, any delay would have then meant walking the latter stages in extreme heat which has its own other sets of problems.

As with all long distance routes that Harry and I have undertaken, we were unsupported and camped wherever legally possible. This method provides freedom but the downside of carrying a 75 litre Deuter rucksack weighing in excess of 50lbs may put many others off.

The route is well marked and offers possibly the most varied long distance trail in Switzerland. Crossing 16 passes in 15 stages, the walker will ascend around 58,000ft; the equivalent of two Mount Everests, and will pass many famous peaks such as the Eiger, Monch and Jungrau, Todi and Titlis and the Wetterhorn.

Cows with ringing bells, dark timber chalets, brightly coloured flowers, cascading waterfalls and quaint remote villages are encountered as one crosses from the German speaking regions into the French speaking zone. The remoteness of Richetli contrasts sharply with the hustle and bustle of Montreux yet all areas are undoubtedly Swiss in character and each town, village, pass and remote Alp brings its own charms and unique flavour to this challenging route. The APR is a route that is challenging enough to a well prepared human but imagine attempting this route on all fours; that is exactly what Harry did.

A veteran of long distance routes in the UK; the West Highland Way, Great Glen Way and Raad ny Foillan and also of the Tour du Mont Blanc, this was Harry's greatest challenge. At ten years of age, he was no spring chicken. However, ten years of going up mountains and munros, across bogs and moors, swimming rivers and crossing forests had prepared Harry well. More at home in a tent than in a house, this is one Smooth Fox Terrier who thoroughly enjoys waking every morning and embarking on a fifteen to twenty mile hike.

Weighing in at 11kgs, Harry took the route in his stride despite sub-zero temperatures at the start and 30° heat at the end. Neither sore feet nor frozen fur halted his progress and Montreux was reached successfully and on schedule.

This book recounts Harry's side of the story; his thoughts and experiences as he completed his 250 mile walkies through the Alps. A typical Fox Terrier, Harry is an intelligent and tenacious dog with the character of Donkey from Shrek though thankfully not the ability to talk.

In December 2007, Harry fell 460ft from Striding Edge in the English Lake District. In typical style, he then endeavoured to climb back up to rejoin his 'human' but was too badly bruised and shaken to make it up. Yet within just two weeks, Harry was back to his usual self running around in the winter snows of Liechtenstein.

Me!

MY HUMAN had always been a bit different. I got him when I was 11 months old. Prior to him turning up, my upbringing had been quite sheltered. I had spent the first few months of my life in a wire kennel with my mother and brother. We did not share the same kennel, in fact I lived in the middle one and they lived either side of me. We could see one another and talk but could not touch.

I remember when I first saw my human I knew he was the one. He smiled at me and spoke; he still talks to me all the time. Sometimes it is a bit annoying and I think "For God's sake shut up! Why can't you be like other humans and only say sit or stay?" Other times though it's quite nice and I do think that he genuinely realises that I can understand every word.

At first sight, I stood on my hind legs and gripped the wire mesh with my paws. I sniffed him, I could smell dog. No, I could smell three dogs! Great, a human that has mates for me to play with. The mates turned out to be three Yorkshire Terriers who had two old humans. They did not live with my human but I would get to spend a lot of time with them.

Then he left. I walked back into the hut in my kennel and sulked. I had seen the human I wanted but then he had gone. Why? I wanted that one, he looked really nice.

Two moons passed. Yes, we dogs still have the wolf in us and as we do not have watches, lunar and solar cycles are our way of telling the time. Sometimes I get the time wrong but I blame that on living in England. How can we be expected to know the exact time when it is always so cloudy? Then he came back. What was he playing at? He spoke to the old lady who smelled of stale urine and she opened the door to my kennel. I was hesitant at first, not sure if he had returned because he knew I wanted him or if he was just playing with my emotions. I peered past the old lady, her hairy and varicose veined legs obscured my view but I could still see my human. He spoke to me and I rushed at him. I was excited and wagged my tail so hard that my bum went with it. He reached out and started to rub my head and the backs of my ears. That was cheating! He knew that I would accept him if he rubbed my ears. I would have to be careful with this one; he was wise and knew what I was thinking. I grasped his forearm gently but firmly between my jaws and gently gave a couple of squeezes. That was my way of telling him that I thought he was okay and I think he understood that.

To my surprise and delight, he put a brand new collar and lead on me and I walked him out of the kennel. At last, I had my own human, my very own real walking, talking human! I was so excited that I forgot to say goodbye to my Mum and brother. I glanced back as I walked through the gate into the unknown world and could see that they were happy for me, though I kind of hope they were slightly sad to see me leave. Never before had I passed through that gate. I was an explorer! My ancestors, the wolves would have been proud of me. I knew they were watching and I knew that they would be proud and I would have loved to see the look on their faces. Little me taking a human through the gate into the unknown world; who ever would have thought it?

We got into a car and for my safety the human placed me on the back seat and tied my lead to the door handle. I think he was worried that I would get too excited and distract him or leap on him whilst he was driving. I would not have done that but he was not to know. After all, we barely knew each other and it was his job as my human to ensure my safety and well being at all times. He seemed like a good and well behaved human. I liked him.

I had never been in a car before and this was a new experience. I was slightly nervous but also excited. The trees seemed to whiz by and I occasionally lost my balance as we moved swiftly along the country lanes. At this point I was completely unaware that the car would become a huge part of my life and I would get the opportunity to travel most of Europe as a result.

Now I know that you are surprised; you have probably heard of a Wire Haired Fox Terrier but not a Smooth one and definitely not a one-eyed version. I had a problem with my right eye. It was twice the size of my left. When my human saw this, he took me to the vet and my vet, Mrs Jennings, cut my eye out. I was very brave and although it hurt, I was glad it had gone. My human sometimes laughs at me and calls me "Cyclops" but I know he is only joking. As for my looks, I am just as handsome with one eye as I was with two and humans only look half as silly now but I do wish people would stop saying "He's a big Jack Russell". I am NOT a Jack Russell! Neither am I some sort of cross-breed, at least not until someone does not know what I am! I also wish that people would be more considerate when approaching me as I sometimes panic if I am approached from my blind side, I also sometimes bump into things and humans find that amusing too even though it hurts my head.

I thought that Mrs Jennings was a sadistic descendant of Dr Frankenstein when I first met her as she immediately wanted to dissect me. However, I now realise that she removed my eye for the good of my own health and she was not experimenting on me. I have met many vets since then both at the Towcester Veterinary

Centre and overseas and whilst I do still shake a little, I think they are generally quite nice. Mind you, they do kill some dogs when they get old. That happened to two of the old Yorkshire Terriers I knew.

Dusty was a bit smelly and very old and Kim seemed a bit scatty. Both had known my human for their entire lives and Kim told me lots of stories about how my human had taken her on long walks up big mountains in all weathers when she was younger. Both had long lives and Dusty was "put to sleep" as the humans say when he was almost eighteen and Kim was fourteen. I hope my human does not ask the vet to kill me when I get too old to walk.

That all happened many years ago and since then, I have explored Scotland, the Lake District, the Isles of Scilly, Wales, the Peak District and just about every other corner of the British Isles that you can mention. My lucky human has been shown the whole country by little old me. However, now it was time for something different. No more walking up Scottish hills in the snow. I was to become an experienced mountain dog. I have taken my human up Ben Nevis in the winter snows, walked him from Corrour Station across the peat bogs, climbed the highest mountains in England, Scotland and Wales and led him to safety in the fog on Cadair Idris, Striding Edge, Sharp Edge, Quinag and Canisp. I have also completed a total of five years Waendel Walks consisting of 25 miles per day along footpaths and roads in Northamptonshire and the Blankenburg two day event; I even have the medals to prove it. My human and I have also walked the Great Glen Way, West Highland Way and Raad Ny Foillan. After all of that, I ended up going into Europe and walking the Tour du Mont Blanc and many miles of paths around Zermatt and Chamonix. However, this all led to my toughest ever challenge. It was a challenge that I would look forward to and thoroughly enjoy. I was to walk from Sargans to Montreux along the Swiss Alpine Pass Route!

We set off at the end of May in 2006, just over two months after my tenth birthday. I saw my human loading the car and knew that we were going away. He had told me several times that we were "going on holiday", "staying in a tent" and that "it will not be like any other holiday you've ever had". I watched intently as rucksacks, boots, the tent, walking poles, crampon, ice axes. Ice axes! Snow? My memory flashed back to my winter walking in Scotland; trudging from Glen Nevis up to the top of Ben Nevis or through Glen Coe and the Lost Valley. It had been great fun but I only have small feet and that allows me to sink into soft snow. Now I do not want to go into graphic detail but there are certain parts of my anatomy, three in particular that I am very proud of and do not enjoy dragging through snow or across ice. Yes, I do have all my bits. I nearly did not but one day when I was at the vet I heard my human say "At forty pounds each, he can keep them". That was a good day for me.

Then something strange happened that left me confused and somewhat worried. We went to bed. Would this be the same as the time he went to Canada or to Tanzania? On those occasions he loaded his car and went to bed then drove off the next day without me. Do not worry I was not left home alone. Although even if I had, I would have been okay. I could have watched Wildlife on One and read my back issues of Play Dog; Poodle of the Month was always my favourite! No, I was always left with the wrinkly humans and three Yorkshire Terriers. After Kim and Dusty had been killed, the wrinkly humans only had Ben so they got two more dogs; Meg and Bonzo. I like the Yorkies though Ben is grumpy, and Meg has this weird habit of grinning when she gets nervous. It is very funny but not at all dog like. I have heard that she comes from Manchester and that is why she is a little odd. I am not one hundred percent sure where Manchester is but I think it must be in a different solar system as Meg is very strange. She sometimes swears a lot and I think that must be because she comes from Manchester too as Noel Gallagher is always swearing.

The wrinkly humans are okay. They feed me, walk me, take me out in the car and sometimes fuss me. They are also a little strange though as they have removable teeth. Do not ask me why, they just do and it is scary enough when a human shows their teeth so just imagine what it is like when they take them out. I have nightmares of their teeth climbing out of the glass during the night. As the Steradent drips from the shiny plastic they chase after me gnashing at my bum as I run and hide. It really is far too frightening and just writing about it makes me tremble with fear.

Off to bed we went and I lay waiting and wondering. Would he take me? Would he leave me? If he left me, would he come back? If he came back, would he still want me? Was there another dog that my human was taking? My mind was racing. Could my human be taking another dog? Was I to be replaced by a Bassett Hound or maybe a Puli? I hoped not. I had absolute faith in my human and was sure that he would not replace me but I was getting older and you just never know. Humans are strange and sometime callous creatures hence we are in the middle of a mass extinction of species caused by human activity. If I had still been in possession of both eyes, I would have kept one open to observe what was going on. I decided that I really should get some sleep so kept my good eye closed and watched through my missing one. I had heard that a famous English admiral once looked for ships through his missing eye and thought it would be noble of me to do the same.

Finally, just as the sun was rising and the morning dew was evaporating from the grass in the Sun's first warmth, my humans alarm clock rang. It was time, it was far too early in the day for waking but it was still time to get up. He spoke to me, lifted me onto his bed and started to stroke me. Was he saying goodbye or good morning? I was not too sure and was very suspicious. That was it!

LLOYD P. CLARK

I would follow him around the house, staying as close as I could and not allowing him out of my sight for a single moment.

Slowly he got dressed. I was already dressed and wearing my very best fur coat. A quick shake and I was ready. Off we went down the stairs. My human was in front and I was one eighth of an inch behind. Damn, the Yorkshire Terriers were up as well and the wrinkly humans. I still had no idea whether he was taking me or leaving me. Off he went into the bathroom and then something really worrying happened. The male wrinkly clipped my lead to my collar and took me out along with the Yorkies. Would my human be there when I got back? I had one last sniff at the foot of the bathroom door and as I was dragged out of the house, I studied the car.

We have a burgundy coloured BMW and I could just see bits of luggage poking up into view through the windows. The car was clean and shiny but covered in nocturnal condensation. There was a slight chill in the air but the warmth of the sun added a pleasant ambience to the atmosphere. As we walked, I glanced back a few times until eventually I could just see the tailgate of the car as I rounded the first corner. The village was still and quiet as we walked across the street and entered a short stretch of tarmac footpath.

I had walked this path a thousand times. There was a mixture of aromas. Dogs, cats, humans, horses, foxes and rats had all used this route over the past twenty-four hours though it was the pungent smell of foxes that captured my senses. Both a female and male had passed by quite recently and I could tell that they had headed toward the nearby allotments. We were heading in the same direction and as I cocked my leg in an effort to leave my scent, I hoped that the foxes would make themselves visible.

As the warm yellow liquid flowed from me across the new grown nettles, a slight steam arose from it showing that my body was slightly warmer than the surrounding air. "C'mon Harry" said the wrinkly old man as he pulled my lead. He tugged at my collar and nearly wrenched my head from my neck. "Miserable old wrinkly" I thought as I continued leaving my scent. Why should I hurry? I had been in bed all night and was just performing the joint task of leaving my scent and emptying my full bladder. Would he have preferred me to do it on the carpet? I think not though I have noticed that he occasionally misses the toilet and splashes the wall and carpet; some of these humans have such unhygienic ways.

Eventually I finished and we continued on our way. Just as we reached the allotments, we turned left through a gap in the tall hawthorn hedgerow and into a field of wheat. Leaving the tarmac behind, the ground changed to a dry and compact reddish soil. The green wheat contrasted against the ground and swayed gently in a light breeze.

The old wrinkly unclipped my lead, I was free. It was a struggle to resist the urge to run back to my human but I knew that would result in a telling off so I stopped myself and followed the old wrinkly human. The three Yorkshire Terriers followed suit with Meg bossing Bonzo whilst Ben panted behind. Ben is only a few months older than me but is not so fit and hates hot weather. He is actually my best friend out of the Yorkies and though we do sometimes grump at one another we seldom come to blows. Not that it would hurt as he hardly has any teeth.

One lap of the field and we were heading back. I tugged and strained on my lead, pulling constantly to get a view of the drive. Would the car still be there? My collar was tight around my neck and I began to cough and choke as I pulled harder and harder. I turned the corner and to my joy and amazement I could see our car. He had not driven away. He had waited for me!

I gave a quick sniff as we walked past the car. It was just a quick one to check whether he had been near the car. He had but I could tell that he had re-entered the house. He was still there and I wagged my tail as the door opened and I walked in. I was still pulling at my lead because that way my nose would enter the house a full hundredth of a second sooner. I strained to see round the open lounge door and there he was, sitting in my favourite armchair waiting for me.

A soon as my lead was detached from my collar I ran at my human and jumped up him placing my front paws on his left thigh. My tail wagging and tongue hanging out of my open mouth, I pushed my head into his hands. Firmly but gently he rubbed my head and then patted my right thigh. He was still drinking a mug of tea and eating some toast. He saved the last piece of crust for me and held it out towards my mouth. I was grateful for that, in fact I was grateful for any morsel of food except chips. I grabbed the toast between my teeth and with a quick flick of my head it was in my mouth where I began to chew it. The toast was slightly dry but came with butter which gently melted around my mouth filling it with a light creamy taste. A quick swallow and it was gone but so was the rest of the toast.

"Are you ready?" he asked me. Of course, he knew I was but he also knew that I was not too sure what was happening so he gave me a reassuring rub on the head as he got up out of the chair. He walked over and opened the front door, "Come on then, in the car" he stated. I was a bit uncertain; I wanted to go but was not sure whether he really meant for me to leave the house. He then said "Come on Harry, get in the car". I ran out of the house, jumped off the front door step and ran up the path alongside the drive. At the top of the path, I turned and stood attentively at the rear of the car. With a dull click and a flash of orange light from every corner of the car, the doors automatically unlocked. My human walked to the rear of the car and with another click, the tailgate was open. He reached up, took hold of the rear wiper and raised the tailgate. I stood rigid and excited, my mouth open, my tongue hanging out and my eye glistening in the early morning sun. My human reached down and took hold of me with both hands. He lifted me into the boot of the car before saying "Stay there". He then reached up and again took hold of the tailgate and firmly closed it. That was it, I was in the boot. I was going on holiday!

My human walked down the drive and opened the car door. Lowering himself in, he sat behind the steering wheel and inserted the ignition key. The door closed and he started the engine, with a deep vroom all six cylinders roared into life. I watched the wrinkly old lady as she stood in the doorway, her plastic teeth were glistening in the early morning light and her silver hair fluttered lightly in the breeze.

She waved goodbye. "Be careful and enjoy yourselves" she stated. How stupid did she think we were? Why wouldn't we be careful? And why wouldn't we enjoy ourselves? When I was younger it was a different story and I once decided to leap over wet rocks in Glen Nevis. Upon landing I slid helplessly backwards down a smooth wet rock. I fought to regain some form of grip, my claws scratched and scrapped as I tried with all my strength to climb up the rock. Gradually I moved upwards but then I slipped again and plunged backwards over the edge. I fell around twelve feet and landed on a tiny ledge. Two hundred feet below me the foaming waters of the River Nevis were waiting to batter me against the eroded boulders that had succumbed to her forces.

I stood helpless and quivering. I barely dared to move as I knew I was close to certain death. If the fall did not kill me the icy roaring river most certainly would. I looked worriedly for a way up. I could see my human looking down at me. "You dumb animal" he shouted. "Stay there". Did he really think I would even dare to go anywhere? I watched as he removed his rucksack and carefully began to climb down. The rocks were loose and wet. I knew that he would be struggling for grip and just hoped that he would hold on.

Finally he stood by my side. The rock we were on was barely big enough for our six feet. Carefully he bent down and told me I was a good dog. As he cautiously balanced he lifted me up. I held my breath; if he dropped me now I would die. As he lifted me he stood up and slowly raised me above his head. He placed me on a narrow ledge. As he climbed upwards he kept his right hand placed against my body. The ledge was too narrow for me to stand on unaided.

As my human moved higher, he placed one of his feet on the ledge. His position was awkward and unsafe. He held onto a sapling with his left hand and was leaning out and down to ensure his right hand was pinning me against the rock. Slowly his right hand began to move. I prayed the sapling would hold and that its young roots were bedded firmly into the tight crevasses in the granite. I felt my humans' fingers grip my collar and before I could stop him, my human hauled me upwards. My collar tightened on my neck and I choked momentarily before being placed slightly higher up.

I was only a couple of feet from the top and felt I wanted to do the rest on my own. As I moved, my human gruffly shouted "Stay there!" I froze. My heart raced and my breathing slowed. Nervously I licked my lips.

My human moved up further. My ledge was slightly wider this time and he was able to let loose of me momentarily. Fear kept me motionless until once again my collar was grasped and I was swung upwards like and old sack. My human released his grip on my collar and the momentum of the swinging action flung me sideways onto the footpath. I had survived. I watched intently as my human completed his climb. He had saved me, I had survived! I jumped at him excitedly as he stood on the path and ran back and forth wagging my tail. As we walked back towards the car I stayed as far from the edge as I could. I had nearly died but my human had saved my life. I would sleep very contentedly that night but even now I have occasional flashbacks. I think they call it post traumatic stress disorder.

Gently the car moved backwards and I wagged my tail as I panted and jumped around in the boot. I was very excited but knew I was in for a long drive. Just how long, I was not sure but he did say that it would be longer than Scotland. I was not worried as I would sleep for some of it.

The Journey

As we drove away from the village, he was talking to me. "Okay Harry, you're on holiday now. We'll drive to Dover, catch a ferry and then drive through Holland, Germany and into Switzerland. Then we'll walk from Sargans to Montreux". I was not too sure what he was talking about and questions began to race through my head. Where is Harwich? Why were we not going from Dover or through the tunnel? Why do all the dykes live in Holland?

Mrs Jennings had said that I needed to be vaccinated against rabies to go to these countries. She said that rabies makes you go mad, drink lots of water, foam at the mouth and bite people. It did not sound very nice. As for biting people, I have bitten one person, the old wrinkly man and he did not taste too good. I think he tasted strange because he was so old and starting to go rotten. If humans have a sell by date, he was definitely past his. Maybe I should try something younger and prettier? Where does Keira Knightley live?

As we headed into the sun, I was glad to be in the back of the car. The sun was very low in the sky and was dazzling my human. I did not see this as a major problem though as the sun was going to rise in the sky and in any case, we were in England, the cloud would soon obscure the sun.

The radio was playing as we progressed past Northampton and out along the A45. It was comforting to hear the voice of Richard

Allinson and the various songs playing as I lay down to sleep my way across the country, it certainly was "the best time of the day".

The rear seats had been laid down in the car and through my dog guard (a sort of wire mesh barrier that prevented me from lying on the seats). I could see our luggage and the left arm of my human. I lay curled in a ball, listening to Dido and watching my human just to make sure that he did not curl up and doze. As comfortable and obedient as the car is, it has not yet learnt to drive itself. There was the occasional rattle of metal as bits of luggage moved around as we negotiated roundabouts and hit the numerous bumps and holes in the road surface. The car was moving swiftly and we seemed to be passing everything else travelling on the road, not that there was a lot of traffic as most humans and dogs were still asleep.

I had been asleep for a while, do not ask me how long as I do not wear a watch but the sun was higher in the sky and Sarah Kennedy was on the radio. Suddenly the car slowed. I got up and looked out excitedly. "Are we there yet?" I thought. No such luck. We were queuing in traffic. Cars, lorries and vans were all around us. My human turned the car stereo down slightly as there was no longer as much wind or engine noise to drown the sound.

I waited patiently in the back for a motorbike to pass. I like doing that. I sit watching out the back for them to come driving down between the lanes, weaving their way through the traffic. As they approach I sit perfectly still, waiting. Quickly they get nearer and I lower my stance whilst slightly raising my hind quarters. Then as they draw level, I pounce, slamming my front paws against the side of the car and giving a single "Woof!" Okay, so now you are thinking me a little odd. Do you not know just how fearsome bikers can be? For starters they ride along draped in dead cow. In fact I have seen one female biker who was so large that she generated her own climate and had to wear several dead cows! And they have one huge rectangular eye and no hair. If I did not defend my territory they would grab me and rip off my head, drain the blood from my body and discard my corpse for the crows to eat. I do a good job of frightening them off as none have ever grabbed me, ripped off my head, drank my blood or thrown me to the crows. I can scare any biker.

Whilst protecting myself from passing motorcyclists, I also had a brief look around. Were there any dogs in passing vehicles? Any animal's in nearby fields? Was there anything else of interest? The answer was a very simple no. This was in fact Cambridgeshire, home of the sugar beet and they are not known for beauty or animalistic behaviour.

Thankfully, soon the traffic was moving and the surrounding land was becoming increasingly hilly. The volume of the radio was increased as we began to speed along the A14. Newmarket; race horses live there. I had been to Newmarket before, in fact I had been most places in the United Kingdom but I had not been to Harwich. I was beginning to wish that I had not had those extra few laps of water before we left. I was starting to get desperate and without thumbs, you cannot tie a knot in it. Not that I would want to, whatever would I do if I could not untie the knot? It would go blue and fall off like a docked tail and no-one would ever know whether I was a dog or a bitch.

Pretty soon the car pulled over to the side of the road and drew to a halt. My human alighted and walked toward the rear of the car. Was this our destination? I hoped not as there was nothing here. We'd stopped in a lay-by with nothing to sniff other than a couple of straggly hawthorn bushes with old torn carrier bags dangling in them, flapping and rustling every time anything larger than a transit van passed by. Old plastic coke bottles littered the short section of pathway and a dirty grey coloured Ford Mondeo estate car was parked behind us with an overweight sales executive sat at the wheel. He was reading a copy of The Sport and eating his breakfast, I could almost taste the bacon.

I jumped around in the rear of the car, wagging my tail and looking as excited as any excited dog could ever look. My mouth was open, my tongue flailing around and odd spurts of saliva shot from my mouth splattering against the windows. My human walked to the back of the car and opened the tailgate. "Stay there" he exclaimed as he lent in and clipped my lead onto my collar. Then, grabbing the tops of my fore legs, he lifted me out of the car and placed me on the ground. At this point I realised that this was just a quick stop to allow me to cock my leg. My bladder was full to the brim and felt like a space hopper but I could not go with all the vehicles passing. Would he want to go in front of passing cars, coaches or lorries? I doubt it and I was the same. I pulled towards a small clump of bushes. I wanted to see what smells I could find and keep away from the huge rumbling trucks as they thundered past only feet away from me.

We walked to the rear end of the lay-by and then turned and headed back for the car. I decided that there was only one thing to do and half heartedly raised by left rear leg against a tall thistle. I was relieved and I knew that it would keep him happy and I would be allowed back into the car to continue our journey. I was correct, as we approached the car there was a flash of orange light as the doors unlocked and I was lifted back into the car. I jumped around a little as my human opened his car door and lowered himself into the seat. The engine started and we quickly accelerated out into the carriageway. I looked out of the rear as a huge Scania truck began to bare down on us though I need not have worried as we were soon pulling away from it as the car bounded down the road.

Sniffing the air I began to notice an aroma of salinity. Were we approaching an industrial complex or the sea? The smell did not go away it got stronger. We were going to the seaside! I love the beach. Running through the edge of the breaking waves with warm, golden sand under my pads was something that I had not done since a trip to Wales earlier in the year. I loved the sea and during my time I have paddled in the North Sea, Irish Sea, Atlantic Ocean, English Channel and the Mediterranean.

We soon came to a series of roundabouts. I dug my feet in hard against the floor as the car swung left, right, left offsetting my balance and causing me to lean as gravity tried to pull me first to one side of the car and then the other. Occasionally, I have a roll in the back of the car and kick my legs in the air as I wriggle on my back, a roundabout will approach unexpectedly and I suddenly find myself rolling helplessly across the boot. This time though I was alert and well prepared. I stood firm as we entered an industrial estate. Unattended lorries were parked in rows behind a tall chain-link fence. The smell of salt water was strong and gulls were calling overhead as we slowly manoeuvred toward a small hut with a woman sitting in it.

Okay, this is the bit where I bark to stop the plump lady entering the car. After a few woofs my human told me to "shut up". My human could be very rude to me sometimes! He handed over some bits of paper to the woman and she gave him a form to fill in to state that he was with a dog. What was this place? Why did he need to fill in paperwork? Surely he was not selling me, I had not been that bad, had I? He never had to fill forms in about me at Dover or the tunnel.

He thanked her and she told us to enjoy our trip as a red and white striped arm was raised from in front of the car and we drove through. Turning sharply to the right we were directed into a long row of other cars and, as we approached the rear of a Volvo, we stopped.

I looked around curiously. This was a bit like a car park but people were staying close to their cars. There was a car with two big humans next to us and they had children with them, one boy and one girl. The girl pointed at me and said "Look at that dog". What was her problem? Had she never seen a one-eyed Smooth Fox Terrier before? She probably had not as there are not that many two-eyed versions around, let alone one-eyed versions. I looked back at her and pulled a few scary faces. No one else noticed but I think she found them funny, particularly the ones where I put my paws in my mouth and pull out the corners, as I do so I stick out my tongue. It is difficult to do but entertaining to others.

Again I was lifted from the car and was slowly walked up and down the length of the car park constantly being encouraged to cock my leg. I tried but I could not go, not whilst everyone was watching me. Up and down we walked and lots of people stopped, stared and pointed at me. I began to wonder whether I had something stuck on me. I checked but there was nothing. I soon realised that I was a novelty because there were no other dogs in the car park and then heard a male human ask "Are you taking him abroad?" My human explained that he was and that it was not my first time. He said that I had been vaccinated against rabies and that I had a passport. I remember the wrinkly female human being very upset that my human had asked her to have my photo taken for a passport but I was not too sure what a passport was. He was joking as I did not need a photo but she had taken him seriously and was planning to take me to a photo booth!

We continued walking up and down until I was very, very bored. Just as I was about to complain, a loud noise came over a speaker and a woman's voice exclaimed "Please return to your vehicles, the ferry will be boarding in five minutes." Quickly I was taken back to the car, placed in the boot and the car engine started. This was a bit strange because everyone in the car park had done the same. All I could hear was the noise of starter motors turning and engines bursting into life as the smell of un-burnt petrol and carbon monoxide filled the air.

We remained stationary as the row to our right moved away. Then I watched as the car in front moved off, followed by us and then the cars behind. Like a long metal snake we filed through the car park up onto a spiral concrete bridge. Then I saw it. A huge metal boat with its enormous mouth gaping wide open. Cars, lorries, motorbikes and coaches were all driving straight into the metal boats mouth. I was a bit nervous as we entered it. I felt a bit like a canine Jonah entering the belly of a huge metal whale and wondered whether we would ever get out or be slowly digested as it toured the world searching for more prey.

The lighting began to fade as we drove into the mouth and I could hear the wheels making a different sound as the tyres began to grip on the rough metal floor. The air was warm and thick with carbon and Terry Wogan began to crackle on the radio. Suddenly the car titled upwards, nervously I swung round to see what was happening. We were driving up a long metal ramp onto another level. At the top, the car turned left and we parked behind a small red car.

My human switched off the engine and got out. He walked to the rear door of the car, opened it and took out my water bottle. It was a new, transparent blue water bottle with an integral dark blue bowl. After unscrewing the bottle from the bowl, he poured me some water, opened the boot and allowed me to have a drink. This was no time for drinking! This was the time to leap into the belly of the boat and run around sniffing and cocking my leg. Alas I was not allowed out. I just had to stand in the boot having my ears rubbed until eventually the boats belly was full of vehicles.

As the last person left the car deck, my human told me to "Be a good boy" before closing the boot and locking me in. With a click and three flashes of orange light, I was locked in this warm and strange smelling environment. The aroma of oil and carbon monoxide left a pungent smell as I listened to the boat growling gently, its turbine engines barely operating as we sat motionless in the water. As I wondered how long this would last and how we were managing to stay afloat, I watched my human disappear into a nearby doorway. I was alone, warm and worried.

As I sat wondering what to do with my time, the turbine engines roared into life. The sound was dull and muffled as the ship and its cargo began to vibrate and rattle. I could sense movement a bit like that you experience in an elevator. I had only ever been in an elevator a couple of times but that was strange, I went up and my stomach forgot to come with me, then it caught me up a split second after I had stopped. I began to notice a slight roll as we gently rocked from side to side. What happens if I get sea sick? Well, I guess I would be able to bring up my breakfast and then eat it again. At least the second time my biscuits would be warm and soft, kind of partially cooked.

Okay, this was getting silly. For over three hours, I had been sitting in the belly of this boat twiddling my claws waiting for my human to come back. The rolling sensation had got slightly worse and the noise levels had increased. The smell of oil was now starting to make my eyes and throat feel uncomfortable. I needed a drink and I needed the loo. Maybe if I lay on my back and was a good aim, I could open my mouth and satisfy both needs in an acrobatic way; on second thoughts maybe not. Warm drinks are not really my thing. I wonder how many dogs have experienced sitting in a metal box within a metal box with hundreds of feet of water below them.

As the vibration and noise began to subside, my human appeared from the doorway. I wondered what he had been doing. I reckoned he had fed himself. As he opened the car, I could smell chicken, chips, vegetables and milk. I hate that. I had been abandoned, left to fend for myself and guard the car and he had been off stuffing himself. Then he allows me to smell the aroma of food as it drifts from him. What did I get? Water nothing more, nothing less. Just luke warm water. I drank it as fast as I could. My throat was dry from the fumes and warm air that I had been breathing for the past three and a half hours. I needed to empty my bladder and my bowls but he disregarded that and closed the boot. I was trapped again but this time he got in the car with me as all the other humans returned to their vehicles.

Engines began bursting into life whilst headlights and brake lights began illuminating all around me. "Well Harry, as we drive down the ramp, you'll be entering Holland". I knew that Holland was a flat place and wondered when I would get to walk on it. As the car in front pulled away, my human drove our car along the deck. Turning slightly, we started down a metal ramp and emerged into bright and dazzling sunlight. I squinted slightly as the sun hurt my eye following nearly four hours in the dull lighting of the boats belly. At last fresh air was able to enter my nose and lungs. We drove across a large area of tarmac, crossed some railway lines and turned right into an empty car park. We drove right to the far end towards a large red and white lighthouse and then stopped.

I was now allowed out of the car. At last, just as my bladder was about to burst and my bowels were on the verge of erupting, I was allowed to get out and run around. I ran aimlessly for a few seconds, stretching my aching legs and breathing the fresh sea air before cocking my leg and attempting to flood Holland. Then I made the largest hill in sight as I emptied my bowels for the first time on foreign soil. What a relief. Now all I wanted was to explore this new flat land, to see some windmills and some dykes wearing clogs. To my surprise, disgust and amazement, my human scooped me into his arms and placed me back into the boot. He then closed it, got in the car and we drove out of the car park.

What was happening? We had made it to Holland but obviously not to our final destination.

"Another couple of hours and we'll be in Germany" said my human. It was all well and good going to Germany but that was not our final destination, there would still be a long drive ahead of us.

Looking out of the car, I could see lots of flat fields. The houses were at lower levels than the road and big ditches full of water bounded us on either side. Holland looked an interesting place but, from what I understood, we would not be stopping. The sun quickly warmed the inside of the car. Even with the windows open, I was feeling the heat. Panting I leant against my dog guard whilst looking out of the rear window. I was bored and thoughts were flashing through my mind. How much further is it? Are we there yet? I am hungry. Occasionally my human would talk, not to me but to people calling him on his mobile phone. I wished I could have a mobile phone but with no belt to hang it from, hands to hold it or any friends to telephone, it would be pretty useless. Mind you, I would look really cool with a 'dog and bone' and could hang it from my collar but then it may get in my way and could cause a repetitive strain injury in my vertebra.

For some reason, all of the presenters on the radio spoke strange foreign languages. I can never understand what they are saying but people singing on the radio tend to sing in English. My human would not listen to the radio and began listening to his CDs. They are silver discs and when you put them in the radio, people sing. I do not like many of the songs they sing and sometimes wish that I could put my claws in my ears. Instead I just have to put up with it and try to sleep when I can.

The journey was long and though my human would sometimes talk to me, most of the time he was quiet. I was still bored as he said "Now you are in Germany". If it was not for the big sign-post, no-one would ever know. Everything looks just the same. The grass is still green, the cows are still black and white and the buildings still look the same as those in Holland. It was getting quite hilly though and we were going faster in the car. Well, we were going faster until we got stuck in a traffic queue. Traffic queues are really boring. Going along at walking pace in a long line between other cars is far from exciting. I do have some fun looking at the funny humans on either side. Some stare at me and point but I think most humans never notice me.

It was hot in the car but for some reason he only opens the windows when we are going slowly. I think he dislikes the wind-noise that is generated by open windows. However, I do have a cunning trick. You see, he also dislikes the smell that my bottom makes when I pass wind. In particular, the ones that burn as they come out seem to really upset him and the instant I do that, the windows open. So, every time I want some fresh air, I fart. It can sometimes be difficult to push one out and, if I need a poo, I have to be careful that only the gas comes out but it is very effective.

Occasionally, I walk around or have a roll in the back of the car when my legs were getting stiff and I need a bit of exercise. I had been in the car for ages and the sun was now on my right. I knew that soon it would start to get lower in the sky and the car would cool down. When and where would we stop? When I got bored with walking in small circles, I would throw my pigs' ear up in the air and have a chew of it. It tasted nice, slightly salty and a bit greasy but it was like chewy bacon. The ear I had was quite hairy and had big veins on it that would occasionally get stuck between my front teeth. It meant I had to shake it loose and I imagined it to be a bit like eating live food.

The traffic began moving again and we quickly accelerated. I could see why we had slowed now, there were men in yellow and orange clothing standing in the road. Idiots! Why could they not stick to the footpath and then we would not have to drive around them. I stared threateningly at them as we went by.

At the end of a very long downhill section, the indicators came on. It was then that it struck me. All through the journey, since we got off the ferry, I knew that something was wrong. We were on the wrong side of the road! We were going to die! Panic and fear took hold of me. I was too young to die, what was this idiot doing? I assumed the crash position and placed my head between my legs. Then I realised, everyone was on the wrong side of the road and the steering wheels on other cars were also on the wrong side. Then I remembered that people in Europe drive on the wrong side of the road. He was not trying to kill us after all. He was just driving where he was meant to drive. I was slightly embarrassed and was unsure as to whether he had noticed my panic. Cunningly I kept my head between my legs and licked myself. It did not need licking but he would not know that.

After indicating for a time, we pulled off to the right and pulled to a halt alongside a petrol pump. My human got out and after taking a metal disk off the side of the car he put a tube into it and started to fill it with petrol. I am not too sure what petrol is but I know that it smells and that the car drinks it. When the cars tank is full, the petrol stops and my human must walk into a building to pay for the fuel. When he does that, I am left locked in the car apparently so that nobody steals me though my human does say that I would be bought back very quickly if I was stolen. After a short time he came back out, got into the car and we drove off. I really wanted to get out of the car but he did not let me. I leapt around a bit but knew that it was futile. We were back on the road and there was no way that he would stop until he was ready. I decided to play I spy.

Playing I spy was boring when you only have yourself to play against. As I have some stuff called Frontline put on me every two months, I had not even got any fleas to talk to or play against. I was alone in the back of the car and I was still bored. Eventually, it became cool enough to sleep so I lay down, tucked my head in against my body and went to sleep.

It seemed like just five minutes later that I felt the car slowing and realised that in the darkness we were stopping at a service station. I looked out at the night sky and could see lots of faint stars and a gibbous moon. The stars are all that remains of my ancestors which is why at full moon, all dogs and wolves should raise their heads to the sky and howl. There is no aggressive meaning in this we are merely talking to our ancestors. I watched the stars for a time as they twinkled in the night sky but then the street lamps within the service area overpowered the light given off by the stars and they were gone.

The car stopped in a parking bay and my human got out and collected me from the rear. Once again I was walked up and down in the service area whilst he encouraged me to relieve myself. It did not take much encouragement. I was desperate to go and as soon as I cocked my leg, it all flooded out. I went several more times before we returned to the car and I was given a bowl of water. I polished that off very quickly and waited whilst the bowl was re-filled with food. "What will it be? What will it be?" I always get very excited at the thought of food. Once again it was crunchy chicken lumps or Eukanuba as he calls it. Dried up, hard balls of meat flavoured stuff. I do not mind it and have looked more muscular since starting to eat it but I can think of better things like real chicken, rabbit or cow. Still I was hungry so I ate it all and gave a big burp at the end which made my human smile. When I had finished, he rubbed the top of my head, closed the tailgate, locked the car and walked into the building. I think he went to get some food. Why can he not have crunchy chicken lumps like me?

I waited attentively in the car, occasionally barking and howling in an effort to stop the car being stolen. This seemed to work as when my human came out, the car and I were still outside waiting for him. Of course, as soon as he came out, I was silent as he thinks I am causing a nuisance if I make a noise. I sat looking very innocent in the back of the car, bolt upright and staring as he approached me. When he got back, I was given another walk up and down the car park and then another bowl of water before being put back into the boot.

This time, when my human got back into the car, we did not drive away. This was very strange. He locked the doors, lowered the rear of his seat and started to go to sleep. I tried my hardest to tell him that there may be a very comfortable hotel nearby with a bed and warm floor for me to sleep on. Unfortunately, he either did not understand or was ignoring me for we remained in the car and he started to snore.

Now how on earth was I meant to get to sleep with him snoring like a pig? Every single breath a huge growl was emitted and on top of that, traffic was roaring along the road nearby. I'd already been in the car for hours, what was he playing at? Why could he not just drive us to our destination so that I could have a proper sleep? As the hours and minutes ticked by, it got colder and darker outside. The night was clear and the air was still and crisp. The temperature inside the car got lower as the warmth drifted off into the atmosphere. I huddled into my red tartan blanket, forcing myself into a tight ball. My fur was insulating my body from the cold night air whilst I gave the occasional shiver in an effort to generate a bit more warmth.

Soon I too was asleep, dreaming of rabbits, foxes and squirrels being chased by a ravenous Harry out catching his live dinner. As I fell further into my dream, I began to twitch and yelp whilst chasing these imaginary creatures.

The night air grew colder and as I lay in the boot, the occasional shiver would run through my body. Initially these created a slight tremble but pretty soon developed into an uncontrollable quiver. Still my human slept. He had told me it would only be for a couple of hours but the new sun would be arriving soon. As I lay I wondered what was going on and occasionally dozed though I also spent a lot of time keeping an eye on what was going on outside. The passing vehicles worried me. The ones on the road were okay but I was not at all sure about the ones that entered the parking area.

As the sun was starting to rise, my human began to stir. After some tossing and turning in the drivers' seat, he awoke and looked around at me. "Are you okay Harry?" he asked. "No, I am cold!" I thought. Then I noticed that he was also shivering and appeared to be feeling the chill. Still wearing yesterday's clothes and the fleece he had worn during the night, he got out of the car and walked around to me. As he opened the boot, he rubbed my head and attached my lead. I was then lifted from the boot and taken for a walk up and down the car park again. We were both shivering as I cocked my leg.

Early morning dew was present upon the long grass at the edge of the tarmac. Despite the cold, I pushed myself into the grass dampening the fur on my legs, chest and stomach. No dogs had wandered this way since I'd last been here but I am sure that a few truck drivers had visited the nearby trees and bushes during the night. I would have to be careful where I put my paws!

Pretty soon we were back at the car and I was given some water and breakfast. Crunchy chicken lumps again. I ate a few but was not very interested. I needed a drink more than anything so when some fresh water was provided, I lapped it down as quickly as my tongue would allow. The water was icy cold and moistened every part of my mouth and throat as it chilled my gullet.

I dearly wanted to have a run but knew that I could not. As I have no road sense, I would probably end up like a hedgehog, flattened and dehydrated with a Michelin pattern across my back. I had to be content with what I'd had and get back into the boot. Reluctantly I allowed myself to be lifted in. My human complained momentarily as he wiped the muck and water obtained from my chest off his trousers. I think he half expected to get wet hands but did not realise I was so dirty. It was not my fault that the Germans have dirty grass and dust in their service areas.

Once again the car engine came to life and we headed off out onto the autobahn. I was getting used to being on the wrong side of the road but was still a little nervous as we set off. My anxiety also stemmed from the fact that this was proving to be a very long journey. I enjoy being in the car but was eager to get out and explore.

As the sun rose, the morning sky turned to various shades of pink and orange whilst dark clouds drifted on the cool breeze. There were many other vehicles on the road but it was quiet compared to yesterday. As the warmth of the cars' heater drifted from the front to the rear, I found myself nodding off to sleep. I tried my hardest to keep my eye open and would occasionally jerk myself awake with a big jolt. Eventually I gave up and with a groan curled myself into a tight ball and with a few licks of my lips and a grind of my teeth I drifted into a deep sleep.

The clicking of the indicators and a slowing sensation awoke me. I jumped to my feet and stood on my hind legs peering through my dog guard and on out of the windscreen. We were stopping at another service area. It was fully light and whilst still chilly, the sun was beginning to warm the air. We pulled into a bay and I was again taken out of the boot of the car. This time was different. As my human yawned he told me that we were going for a quick walk and that I could have some time off my lead. At least that's what I thought he said. His speech was somewhat obscured by the yawn and made him appear to have contracted some sort of speech impediment during the night.

I was correct! My lead was unclipped and at last I could run. We had stopped at an Autobahn Kirk near to Baden-Baden and surrounding it was an open grassy area bounded by trees, shrubs and a fence. I ran aimlessly around stretching my legs out as far as I could and leaping over any potential obstacles. Freedom at last but I knew it would not be long before I was back in the car. This definitely would not be our final destination as we were still on the autobahn. My human mentioned that we would "Be in Switzerland in a couple of hours". That sounded more like it. I knew something of Switzerland; cheese, mountains and chocolate. It was a great place. I had been before and knew I would enjoy it.

I stood momentarily watching some immigrant workers in a nearby field. They were very busy bending and picking vegetables from the soil as a man in a red pick-up truck looked on. I was glad that I was not a worker. The urge to empty my bowels soon distracted me and I headed off to a nearby tree stump. Reversing, I pushed my bum over the top of the stump and strained. Out it popped dark brown and steaming, the vapour carrying my scent on the wind. I felt much better now and joyfully scratched my hind feet against the short grass scattering the green blades and small clumps of soil. Free of my excess baggage, I ran joyfully to my human. After another two laps of the field, I was taken back to the car and loaded into the boot.

I watched with great disappointment as my human walked away from the car. He disappeared into a nearby building. I was annoyed by this as I knew that he was going to eat so I barked momentarily. My barking stopped as red Ford Escort pulled into the bay to my right. Sitting on the rear seat were two very dignified Dalmatians. "Where are the other ninety-nine?" I thought. They looked at me as they sat bolt upright, their noses turned slightly into the air. I stood at my tallest with my front paws on the side of the car as I stretched up on my hind legs. Wagging my tail ferociously, I barked a couple more times. They ignored me! Then it struck me, these were German dogs so probably could not understand my barking as I was barking in English. No. That could not be it. Barking is an international language. They understood, they just thought themselves to be of greater importance than I. That being the case, I would ignore them. Turning my back, I went and sat looking out of the opposite window just glancing back occasionally to ensure that the Dalmatians were still there.

Around thirty minutes passed before my human came back into view. He walked across the car park and unlocked the car doors as he approached the rear of the car. As he opened the boot I could smell food. He had been eating! Luckily for him, he had saved me some food and gave me a sausage to chew. Within a flash I had devoured the snorker faster than Terry Wogan ever could. A single swallow and it was gone and we were setting off again along the autobahn.

The traffic was heavier now and I was really bored. As my human had stated, within a couple of hours, the Swiss border came into site. This was different to the last as we could not drive straight through. A series of tollbooth type huts were strewn across the road and men in uniform were standing outside. The car slowed and my human began fumbling for his passport and my documents. A tall man in a dark uniform approached the front of our car. I stared hard at him willing him to turn away. Quite surprisingly this worked, he just waved at us and gestured that we should continue driving and that we did.

If this was Switzerland, where were the mountains? It looked no different to Germany and smelt just the same. A sort of mixture of countryside and exhaust fumes. We drove through a big city and then returned to the countryside again but were still on a motorway. We rounded a long bend and began descending a hill where my human stopped the car.

We were at another service area but this time a Swiss one. I needed a drink but my water bottle was empty so I settled for a walk. Do not get me wrong, I was looking forward to the walk but after that sausage and a long ride in the car, a drink of water would have been good. We made our way up a bank and onto a small tarmac covered lane and I was able to cock my leg several times. It was important that I left my scent at every service area in case I needed to lead us back to safety. However, it was even more important at this one as I could smell that a number of dogs had recently passed by. At the back of the service area, there was a field and when we got there, I was allowed to run free.

The smells were great but my joy was short lived as my human also needed the toilet. Placing me back on my lead, I was lead down a set of steps and tied to a table at the bottom. I waited patiently as my human went into the building for a few minutes. Glad to be out of the car and somewhere different, I sat contented but alert. Soon he was out and had clearly filled my bottle. I had a quick check to ensure that the contents were cool and clear and not warm and yellow. Thankfully for him, the contents were the former! Back at the car, I had a quick drink and we set off. The heat inside the car was building but I was determined to get some more sleep.

Every so often the car would go dark inside, sometimes for a few seconds and other times for a few minutes. During the longer periods of darkness, the air became cooler but was thick with exhaust fumes. Looking out I could see that we were driving through a series of tunnels. I know a lot about tunnels as I have been a fairly regular passenger on the London Tube.

Thankfully, the countryside was becoming hillier though it was not to be until we had passed Zurich that I would see real mountains. The mountains had trees up to their waist and snow on their tops. I love snow covered mountains!

It was not long before we were pulling off the motorway and after a series of small roundabouts we entered a town. We had crossed the Rhine and were in a new country called Liechtenstein. I was by now very excited as I knew that we were nearing the end of what had been a very long, hot and boring journey.

It was not long before I noticed a couple of dogs and started barking at them. As I did so, my humans' phone rang. It was the wrinkly lady calling him. He did not talk for long as he was busy trying to find where we were going and concentrating on driving through the town. I think I had also annoyed him by barking when I did. Soon we left the town

Before I had realised what had happened, we were up a long straight lane. At the end of it we turned very sharp left and stopped. This was it! We had reached our destination! A field. Not just any old field, this was a field for camping in. We were at Camping Mittagspitx. I could hardly wait to get out of the car.

My human had a brief conversation with a Liechtensteiner. I am not too sure what the problem was but got the impression that they could not understand one another very well. Anyway, it was not long before I was out of the car and tied to a small plum tree. Looking around the field I was unable to see any other tents. There were some small timber chalets dotted up the hillside opposite and a large house behind me. The chalets were made of dark wood and had gently sloping roofs with large eaves but most had small touring caravans parked in them. All appeared empty. Underfoot the grass was soft and short. Small yellow and red flowers were dotted across the grass adding dispersed splashes of colour. A grey tarmac track ran through the campsite and I could hear the nearby sound of cowbells.

My human got the tent out of the car and began setting it up. Our tent was a small purple coloured nylon sheet with no windows and two doors, one on either side. Inside the purple sheet there hung a pale grey nylon bag with a black nylon base. This inner tent was also window-less and had two doors. The tent was just big enough for two humans and a dog so there would be plenty of room for us inside. I had stayed in this one before and found that it does offer good protection from the elements but can be cold inside. I hoped that I would have something warm to lie on otherwise I would only have a thin piece of nylon separating me from the cold and hard ground. That may have been okay for my ancestors the wolves but not for a domesticated dog that was used to living in a centrally heated house.

Within minutes, the tent was up and we headed off for a walk. This would be my first real chance to explore Liechtenstein. I wondered what I would find. Certainly some of the smells were different to anything we get in England but I knew that they were a mix of Chamois and Marmot.

The Cows were ringing their bells as we walked alongside their field and up into the nearby forest. The ground was damp and a warm mist was slowly rising from the spongy forest floor up through the sweetly scented pine trees. It was a pleasant experience and whilst I knew this would only be a short walk and we would soon be going to sleep, I relished every second.

Liechtenstein

A FTER A good long nights sleep, my human announced it was time to explore Liechtenstein properly. The weather was still good as we set off around the surreal Toy Town capital, Vaduz.

Throngs of oriental tourists filled Städtle, the main high street through Vaduz. It was a somewhat strange city. Only 34,000 people live in the entire country with just 5,000 of those living in Vaduz. Everything was clean, tidy and perfectly placed as though we were on a film set. The tourist coaches brought in people who were full of hope and expectation at visiting such a unique and tiny principality yet all were filled with a sense of disappointment at what they found. I was soon to discover that the reason for this was that they all lacked adventure. A swift stop to roam the handful of souvenir shops was nowhere near long enough to discover a country whose main delights were hidden behind a 6,000ft ridge guarded by the fairytale like castle, Schlöss Vaduz.

Always one to go off the beaten track, my human led me up a side street between two restaurants. The smell of food was overwhelming for a constantly hungry dog and I pulled eagerly on my lead to enter one of them. I was not fussy which one, I just wanted to eat! My human kept walking and I had no choice but to follow.

Almost immediately we headed up a steep hill and were soon leaving the tourists and buildings behind and entering forest. Small black squirrels with tufty ears played joyfully on the trees, leaping and chasing one another across the path in front. I tried chasing them but could not mimic their climbing abilities. With me confined to the ground they continued their aerial acrobatics unhindered.

It was not too long before we left the forest and passed by Schlöss Vaduz. Two women, a man and a black Labrador were coming towards us. I was on my lead but the Labrador was running free. She bounded down to me and rolled onto her back urging me to sniff her. I tried desperately to oblige but my human restrained me.

The Labradors humans' caught hold of her and apologised to my human. They all stood chatting for a time. I could tell they were foreign as they had strange accents but they all spoke excellent English and were very polite. After a five minute chat we all said our goodbyes and I led my human into the forest and on to another castle. It was only later that my human realised he had been talking to Prince Hans Adam II von Liechtenstein and his wife. I was most annoyed as I had been denied the opportunity of sniffing the Labradors nether regions and she was a real princess. She even lived in a castle. I am sure that Labrador Smooth Fox Terrier cross breeds would be very handsome too!

After a day wandering the forest above Vaduz and exploring the city itself, we headed back to the tent and my human began preparing for our real walk. I was already tired just thinking about it but I knew I had no choice but to join him. How else would he ever survive?

Whilst he was making our preparations, I met a Swiss couple who were staying in a nearby chalet. They had a West Highland White named Eloy. I liked him and we became good friends. I met Eloy again after our long walk but he did not believe that I had walked all the way. In fact he had the audacity to think I had made it all up. Mind you, Bonzo often accuses me of being a dreamer and claims that there is no way I could ever have achieved my personal altitude record of 12,283ft on Kleine Matterhorn or walked all of the long distance routes as he only has short walks.

Other dogs do not seem to believe me either and just think me a liar when I tell them. It can be quite upsetting but I do realise how it must sound to others. I mean, there's me a disabled Smooth Fox Terrier climbing snow covered mountains, swimming glacial streams and crossing entire countries on foot and then there are the other dogs, walking on their leads in carefully tended parks. Why should they believe that I have seen and done things that they cannot even dream of? I have had a unique life and am very proud of it.

I watched intently as my human packed the rucksack filling it with a lightweight sleeping bag, a single change of clothing, a light weight sleeping mat, Gore-Tex clothing, camera and dehydrated human food. However my food did not go in! This was very concerning as I knew the blue rucksack meant a multi-day walk and I would need my nourishment. I need not have worried. No sooner had I panicked than my human began carefully measuring out my food rations for the walk. I was allowed three handfuls of biscuits a day so I counted and counted and counted. Forty-five handfuls of food! Either I was getting extra rations or he was serious about a 250 mile walk!

As the sun fell in the sky and the temperature dropped, my human and I retired to our tent. Neither of us slept too well that night due to the heavy rain beating down on the tent and the anticipation of what would lie ahead. Was it anticipation or trepidation? I do not think either of us were too sure.

The APR begins

I⊤ WAS the day of our departure. Dawn broke but there was no sunrise. Low cloud obscured any view of the Sun and the temperature was far lower than it had been since we arrived. My human sat in the doorway of the tent as he put his walking boots on. I tried a couple of times to push past him but was not allowed. I would not have run off. I merely wanted to see exactly what the weather was like and to say goodbye to Eloy. Finally he finished lacing his boots and rose to his feet. As I walked from the tent, icy droplets of water ran down the outside of the tent and onto my head. The beads glistened as they ran down to the end of my nose. It tickled slightly so I licked them off.

The grass was wet underfoot and I knew my human would be annoyed at the thought of setting off on our walk with a wet tent. Not only would the tent need to be dried in the evening but it would also be heavier. The weight of our kit was never something to bother me as I do not have to carry anything. I looked around for Eloy but he was still in bed; the curtains of his chalet were drawn and the only sign of life was a faint trail of smoke that rose vertically from the chalet chimney and up towards the clouds. The air was still. The wind that had battered our tent during the night had abated and would mean that the cloud would be slow to clear.

As we made our way towards the toilet block, I pulled on my lead to get to Eloy's chalet. I could smell him but there was no sign of him. I imagined that he would be snuggled into a comfortable bed all warm and cosy. I knew there was little chance of a cosy bed for myself but I would not have swapped places with Eloy for all the bones in Switzerland.

Just a few minutes later and our tent was coming down. My human walked around it in an anti-clockwise direction pulling all but the corner pegs from the ground. The wet material sagged lifelessly under the weight of the water and as he removed two pegs from the front corners, the tent slowly drifted towards the ground. With the final two pegs and the centre pole removed, he proceeded to fold and then roll the tent before placing it in its nylon bag. This was then placed in a thick polythene sack that had travelled with us on numerous other trips, and was then placed inside the rucksack.

I could see that the rucksack was heavy as my human lifted it onto his back. If I had tried to carry it I would have been squashed! My human took hold of my lead and we walked from the campsite. As we departed, he checked the car to ensure it was securely locked. This would be my last chance to see the car for a couple of weeks. I was sad to leave it behind but I knew that it would be safe. My human had made arrangements with Bianca, the daughter of the site owners, to leave the car there. She had laughed at us as she thought it mad to walk over the top of the Alps to Montreux. I must admit that I tended to agree!

We walked along a gravel road towards Triesen Roxy. The road was still and quiet until suddenly hoards of school children came hurtling towards us on their mountain bikes. "Morgan" shouted some whilst others shouted "Gretzi" as they joyfully rode past. These Liechtensteiners seemed far friendlier and far more respectful than their English peers. They all slowed as they rode past us and all were happy and smiling. A couple of fat girls puffed and panted as they tried to keep pace with their slimmer friends. Neither of them spoke as they rode by, every bit of energy and concentration was being directed arduously towards propelling themselves forward as sweat dripped from their brows.

We soon reached the main road. I looked into the Roxy car park to see whether the rotisserie was still there. I had noticed it on Saturday and again on Sunday but today it was gone. The scruffy French man who tended it was nowhere to be seen. I jumped slightly as the bottle recycling bin clattered. It was being collected by a large orange coloured lorry which lifted the bin as we walked past. We crossed the road and waited by a bus stop.

Our walk was to start in Sargans which was a few miles from Triesen so my human had decided to get the bus to there. I had never been on a bus. Trains, tubes, cable cars, funiculars, boats and cars were all familiar forms of transport for me but this would be a new experience though one that I would repeat at the end of our walk.

A lime green coloured single deck bus pulled over to the side of the road. My human and I stepped on board and he tried to pay the driver. I am not sure why but the driver refused payment and insisted that we should find a seat. My human struggled past the seats with his rucksack which was slightly too wide for the central aisle.

The bus was hinged in the middle and we sat in the rear half of the bus. A large disk was positioned in the centre of the bus and I noticed the front and rear sections pivoted around this disk. Whilst my human wanted me to sit near him, I thought it would be more fun to balance on the disk. This was no mean feat and as we bounced and weaved our way out of the principality and into Switzerland I wobbled precariously.

Sargans Bahnhof was our final destination though I must admit that I initially thought we may be getting onto a train. In fact it would be another two weeks before I would get on a train and alight at Sargans. We walked alongside the railway lines on an arrow straight and extremely flat tarmac path. Neatly cultivated gardens accompanied us on the right and up above the castle loomed menacingly on its hillside overlooking the town. Wispy clouds rose from the trees and drifted up the castle walls and over the turrets. I could imagine knights and archers looking down at the local townsfolk ready to attack the marauding hun! This area was steeped in history and the Rhine border of Liechtenstein was measured as one days march for a Roman legion. I imagine that tens of thousands of sandaled feet would have trod the paths we were following as the Roman army retreated under increasing pressure from their German enemies.

It was not too long before we were heading up a steep hill out of Mels and on towards Weistannen. The rain that had disturbed my sleep had cleared and the Sun's rays were quickly warming the ground. This caused a thick mist to rise from the trees and undergrowth. The black tarmac lane we were walking on also had steam rising from its surface. As the tarmac gave way to gravel the concrete houses of Mels gave way to timber chalets balanced precariously on raised stone platforms which clung to the steep hillside.

Much of the route ahead was through steep meadows with lush green grass interspersed with vivid flowers. The grass was still drenched in water which soaked my coat as I pushed my way through. If I strayed from the path my visibility was obscured as the grass was far taller than I.

The forest floors were soft and spongy under paw and I was able to make easy progress. Whilst we were gaining height, the increase was mostly gradual with only a few steep sections. Occasionally we met and crossed a narrow tarmac lane which wound its way upwards in a series of long steeping zigzags.

We took a short rest at a tall wooden cross. The man nailed on it was not real, I imagined that it would be very painful to be nailed on a cross. I had seen these crosses in many places throughout Switzerland. Normally they are placed in a prominent hillside location that allows an impressive panoramic view. I imagined that this one would have been the same when it was initially sited but now the trees had grown tall and any view was lost.

There were many forest scents present and I would occasionally identify a fresh trail. With my nose to the ground I would run sniffing at the trail following the scent in the hope of finding a wild animal at the end. Normally when I followed these trails they would fizzle out though occasionally I would find a marmot, pheasant or rabbit and give chase. However, chase as I might I have never managed to catch any animals except for a lot of frogs one day in Glen Nevis. These proved easy pray and I would gently hold them in my mouth. So as not to crush my new found friends I would hold my mouth slightly open. The frogs felt cold and slimy and would struggle to extricate themselves from the enamelled bars of their new prison. Arms and legs would protrude through the gaps in my teeth until my human managed to pry my mouth open. At this, the frogs would leap from my mouth and hop away into the surrounding bogs. Alas in Switzerland I had no such luck and found no prey.

Despite having walked Raad Ny Foillan just a month earlier, my legs and paws were beginning to ache. This was not due to my age or a lack of fitness but purely down to it being day one of a long trek. Over the coming miles I would adapt to the long daily walks and any aches would shift to being caused by the continual pounding of my paws on loose rocky surfaces. I was not too worried about this as I knew that at the first sight of any pain or damage, my human would stop and place my boots on my paws. I am not keen on wearing boots but they do offer good protection and have served their purpose across Europe.

To take my mind off the aches and pains I began to sing quietly to myself, normally doggy versions of human songs that I had heard on the car radio. In the valley below I could hear the distant sound of a barking sheep dog as I hummed "Then I saw her face now I'm a retriever". As I hummed my tune the barking grew louder and I noticed that we were approaching the home of the barking dog. My human called me over and clipped my lead to my collar. I wear a leather Appenzeller collar with brass cows riveted around its circumference which my human bought for me in Interlaaken. I stopped humming in case my human heard me and began straining at my lead in an effort to glimpse the barking dog.

Suddenly there it was; a somewhat strange looking Pyrenean mountain dog. She was meant to be a sort of off-white colour but looked very tatty and mangy. Lumps of her coat were hanging loose and ready to fall to the ground. Her stance was defensive and though she looked weak and malnourished, I knew that she could be a danger for this was no ordinary bitch. This one had some pups nearby and observed me as a threat.

To my right an old timber barn leant slightly on its subsiding foundations. The door was open and creaked gently on its dry and rusty hinges in the light breeze. I could see yellow straw contrasting sharply against the burnt timber of the barn and gently blowing around in the entrance. Half a dozen playful pups then ran joyfully towards us. Despite being just a few weeks old, they were nearly as big as me and seemed to be struggling with their oversize paws and gangly limbs.

As they stumbled and yapped their way towards us, I noticed the mother lower her stance as her top lip began to rise. I was no threat but she was taking no chances. My human spoke to her and told her to move. She momentarily stood her ground but, upon seeing that he was not intimidated, she slowly moved to walk between us and her brood. I kept a watchful eye on all seven of them. I would have liked to play with the pups but I knew that the mother would attack if I did, so I continued walking but could not help showing my happiness at meeting the dogs.

All six pups and their scruffy mother stood watching us as we gradually walked further away from them and eventually disappeared into the forest. They would be the last dogs I would see for a few days though cows would often accompany us. Pretty soon I was off my lead and as we walked out of the forest and into an area of well groomed fields, I could see Weistannen nestled in the valley ahead. However, I could also see that dark clouds were gathering behind us as a light drizzle moistened the surface of my coat.

The houses were deserted as we passed though all were well maintained and obviously inhabited. The only sound was the distant honking of a post bus and the occasional roar of its straining diesel engine as it negotiated the steep and winding road on the hillside to our left.

The Swiss do not allow anyone to camp except on a registered campsite and there were none in this valley. My human had planned for this and we were booked into a hotel in the town. Upon arrival at the premises we were greeted by a young Swiss girl who spoke no English. My human filled in the guest card and the girl led us to our room. I had stayed in hotels before so I knew to sniff at the bottom of every door as we passed by. All the rooms were unoccupied and it transpired that we were the only guests in the hotel.

Our room was clad entirely in pine. It was clean, bright and obviously newly refurbished. Outside a river crashed and tumbled noisily over the boulders that lay in its bed. The heavy rain of the previous night was making its way from the mountain tops to join the river in Sargans before entering the mighty Rhine. Outside heavy rain was once again falling, making me grateful that we had made shelter in the nick of time. As I settled down on a white sheepskin rug on the floor, my human had a shower and began unpacking the tent. I was a bit confused by this but as he draped it over the shower cubicle I realised that he was drying the tent to make life easier the following day.

I slept soundly as my human memorised the route for the following day. This was a useful ability and meant that the use of a map would be minimal as we progressed across the mountains. When he was confident that he would remember the details of the paths ahead, we went downstairs and into the empty restaurant.

I have an uncanny habit of being able to distinguish a waiter or waitress from a patron and I cannot help but growl at the waiting staff. The humans do not know why I do this and my human in particular gets very embarrassed by this strange habit but my reasons are quite simple. These people are serving up dead animals for humans to eat. Now these are not animals that have died a natural death, they have been professionally slaughtered, dismembered and cooked. My fear is that I may be next; something that could be particularly true when at a Chinese restaurant. Do you know how intimidating it is to know that these people are looking at me and wondering whether I should be sautéed with mushrooms and served on a bed of rice or filleted and grilled with onion rings!

Today's waitress was from Berlin and unlike the Swiss girl, she could speak excellent English. My human ordered his meal and ate heartily whilst I drooled under the table. My drooling being partly the result of the smell of the pork and blue cheese my human was eating but also the temptation of tasting the tall slim Berliner before she cooked me! At the end of the meal I got to try a small morsel of the former prior to us retiring to our room where I had my Eukanuba ration. Whilst I ate, I tried to retain the scent of pork and blue cheese in my nostrils but by the end of my meal those smells were a distant memory. My stomach full to bursting, I consumed a bowl of water and settled down to sleep for the night. Images of the waitress accompanied my snores and helped me into a deeper slumber.

Walking with Death

WHEN I awoke the next morning I was very warm and cosy on the sheepskin rug. I groaned as my human started moving around. My eye followed him for a few seconds and when I was sure he was not ready to leave, I snuggled into a tight ball and sighed a deep groaning sigh.

Though I was curled up and dozing, I listened intently for any sound that may indicate our departure. Eventually my human was dressed, the rucksack was packed and as he lifted it onto his back, I sprang excitedly to life. I jumped to my feet like a coiled spring, gave a big shake and ran to the door. I was so excited that I had forgotten my lead was not attached and was unhappy at the thought of waiting whilst he fastened it to my collar.

Finally the door opened and I pulled vigorously to get us down the stairs as quickly as possible. My efforts were fruitless of course as I am a twenty-two pound dog and my human weighs two hundred pounds even without his rucksack! The restaurant was located at the foot of the stairs and my human ducked below a couple of low beams as we entered it. Once there he removed his rucksack and clipped my lead onto it. Then he made his way to a neatly prepared breakfast table and had his fill of meat and cheese. My mouth was watering as I watched him eat but watered even more when I saw him discretely hide something in a napkin before he left the table.

As we stepped out into the deserted street, the air felt cold and damp. Up on the hillsides, fir trees stood encrusted in snow. This was a totally different scene to yesterday when the trees dark green needles were clearly visible. Light rain was falling as we progressed along the road and stopped by a small church. My human removed the red napkin from his pocket and gave me the two slices of ham and rectangular block of cheese he had saved for me. Without hesitation I took hold of the meat and swallowed it. The ham slid down my throat, barely touching the sides The cheese was too large to swallow so I chewed it and savoured the strong flavour.

The day had got off to a good start and with my breakfast safely stowed in my stomach, we set off. As we reached the centre of Weistannen, the Post Bus was being turned around. I had enjoyed my previous bus ride and wanted to climb aboard this one but my human would not let me. It was still cold and was by now raining very heavily. My human was clad head to toe in Gore-Tex yet I only had my fur to protect me.

Despite the rain we made good progress though I soon started to feel the cold. At first I thought it was just the heavy rain that was making me feel cold but as we walked and gradually increased our altitude, the rain began to fall as sleet. Large wet flakes of snow drifted effortlessly to the ground and thawed upon impact. I quite liked snow so this was a pleasant surprise coming as it did on 31st May. It is common for snow to fall on the summits and high passes at any time of the year but we were only at around 1,200 metres.

The tarmac road had given way to a gravel surface quite some time ago and we had seen no one since Weistannen. Apart from the rustle of my humans Gore-Tex trousers and my name tag tinkling on my collar, our progress was silent. Both human and dog were in unison travelling onwards and upwards through an ever cooling atmosphere and both wondering what lay ahead.

Briefly the rain stopped and the sun broke through the cloud. Snow flakes hanging on the branches of surrounding pines began to thaw and a constant dripping of icy snow melt could soon be heard. Sadly this warmer interlude was very short lived and as the snow resumed so the wind speed increased.

We passed through a farmyard. The aroma of cow manure filled the cold damp air and as we walked between the barns. A couple of horned heads watched us over the low doors that held the cows in their barn. Plumes of thick steam rose rapidly from the cows' warm nostrils and both snorted as we passed by. I could almost here them saying "you'll never make it over the pass in this" but what would they know? After all, a cow is just big leather milk churn that is made into burgers and shoes when it dies. That is no way for an animal to make a living, if you can call dying a living.

Due to the weather I was tending to stick close to my human. The grass either side was long having grown lush in the spring sunshine. Now however, the blades drooped under the wait of the late snowfall and to enter the grass would be extremely foolish for a small dog that needed to conserve body heat. I walked with head and tail lowered moving forward for the sake of doing so and out of faithful necessity rather than as a result of want or need.

Before too long we passed a fairly new timber farmhouse. Unlike other buildings we had seen, this one had clean and bright new timber. Children's toys were strewn across the garden and a lone swing hung heavy with wet snow. I imagined that the children must be tucked away somewhere warm and dry and longed to be with them. Alas I was not to join them and the house was soon a small speck below us remaining barely visible as the snow began to fall more heavily.

No longer was the snow thawing. A thickening white carpet lay ahead and the red and white bergweg markers became increasingly difficult to spot. My human seemed able to stay on the path by following a sinuous depression in the ground. The snow was still wet and made the ground slippery underfoot. A couple of times my human stumbled cursing and moaning due to the load on his back.

Thick icy snow lay in the corries and occasionally blocked our progress forcing us to climb over them. Mostly my human was able to walk on top of the frozen snow but sometimes he would fall through up to his knees. Getting out of such deep snow was awkward with a big pack on but impossible when he finally went through up to his waist. I watched in concern as my human first removed his pack and then used his hands to lift himself from the hollow.

Walking across the frozen snow was dangerous even when it was able to support my humans' weight. The new snow was unable to grip on the icy stuff below and occasionally would slip away as he walked over it. Small avalanches carried the snow down from where we disturbed it. Hundreds of feet below, the snow cascaded into the icy river. My lower weight and claws enabled me to pass over quite acrobatically but my human could not emulate such finesse. In order to make life slightly safer, he placed crampons on his boots and we soldiered on past tumbling waterfalls, across snow bridges and under cliffs. A chamois watched inquisitively as if to ensure that we were not hunters. Chamois hunters are rare but there are still some out there. As we moved closer, the chamois would effortlessly spring their way up the surrounding rocks and snow before disappearing into the clouds.

Having passed a large waterfall we reached a more level area. This was Foo Alp and a lone building could be seen ahead through the snow. Unfortunately between that and ourselves lay a raging and swollen torrent of water. The bridge that should have provided a crossing point had not been assembled for the summer; bridges are often dismantled and stored near to their crossing point to prevent winter flood damage. Partially submerged stones were visible but the current was far too strong for my human to risk crossing on their ice covered tops.

Having spent a few minutes wandering up and down the bank of the river, my human eventually decided upon the safest crossing point. It was safe for him but far too deep for me to paddle across and too fast flowing to risk swimming. I hoped that he would not carry me as that did not look too safe but I could see no other way over. The next thing I knew was my lead being clipped to my collar with the other end clipped onto a Charlet Moser attachment on my humans' rucksack belt.

I pulled back as he waded out into the freezing waters. His feet were submerged with the water up to his knees; his feet must have been soaking and frozen by the icy water. Try as I might I could not dissuade him and before long I was forced to lunge into the raging torrent. I swam with all my might but to no avail, the icy current took hold of my body and pulled me downstream. My collar tugged hard on my neck as my lead became taught. I prayed that the lead would not become loose or worse still that my head would not slip through my collar. I paddled hard and held my nose as high as I could out of the water. My ears were all that prevented my collar sliding off my head. I could feel the cold sapping the heat from my body and my strength diminishing.

Thankfully my human soon reached the other bank and hauled me out of the water. He called me a good dog and patted me before unclipping my lead. As soon as I was free, I began running as fast as I could to dry out and regenerate some body heat. This activity had its own dangers as I slipped and stumbled over snow and ice covered rocks. My human was now sitting down draining the water from his boots and wringing out his socks. His feet looked frozen as he re-laced his wet boots. Just a few yards from us, the river fell almost a hundred feet over a waterfall. The foaming water disappeared into a haze of spray and falling snow. I was grateful that my lead and collar had held so that I was not washed over the waterfall but I was certain that my neck had been somewhat stretched.

We both had a small amount of chocolate before moving on. As we walked onward and upward towards the head of the pass, my human would stop momentarily to regain his breath and to brush the snow and ice from my coat. The higher we climbed the windier and colder it got. Pretty soon the wind was blowing uphill from behind us. As snow fell from the sky, spindrift blew up and attached itself to my bare bum. One of the hazards of having a tail that sticks up is a bare bum revealed to the elements and I would imagine that upon crossing the pass, my bum was a baboon-like red and blue colour. How I longed to warm it by the fire. My humans' glasses kept icing up and snow was encrusted upon his eyebrows.

I imagined that Foo Pass would be a lovely place in the correct weather conditions but today stopping would have meant risking hypothermia. We reached the summit but with no hesitation we began our descent. The path was barely visible and my human slipped and stumbled his way downhill. Finally he took a big tumble. Thankfully I saw him bearing down on me and I managed to leap out of the way. He hit the ground hard then slid and rolled a short distance before coming to rest on his back with his feet facing uphill. The snow had undoubtedly cushioned his blow but he had still taken a bad tumble.

Try as he might he could not get up. I watched with concern as my human flailed around like a fat person too large to touch the ground with his arms or legs. In the end he gathered his thoughts and unfastened his rucksack so that he was able to roll off it and onto his feet. He brushed the snow from his clothing and limped around for a few minutes as if trying to establish whether he was damaged or not. Thankfully he was not badly damaged, just slightly bruised and grazed, though he was annoyed at having ripped his PacLite trousers. My human could heal but his trousers would not.

With his rucksack secured on his back, we carefully continued our descent. I kept my distance in case he fell again but it did not happen. Our descent was slightly more sheltered from the wind and before long the dry powdery snow we had experienced on the summit started to give way to increasingly larger and wetter flakes. The temperature had also risen from sub-zero to one or two degrees above freezing and my fur soon became ice free though was still extremely wet.

With the wet snow hanging in the long grass and both of us soaked and cold, camping out was not an option. To do so could have had fatal consequences so my human decided to aim for an alp building. Death had walked with us over the pass and at one point was so close that I am certain I could see his footprints in the snow and feel the coolness of his breath on the back of my neck but we were determined to leave him behind. Our determination swung from completing the walk to surviving the day; the alp building was our only option. We both walked with determination towards the building and Death decided to follow a different path to that which we now trod. We had defeated him on this occasion but I knew he was still keeping a watchful eye on our progress.

The building appeared deserted as we approached but thankfully it was occupied. Neither of us had the energy to continue much further. The day had been long and far harder than planned. To continue further would have sapped the remainder of our energy and left us too tired for the morning. My human opened the door to the alp building and the warm air inside rushed out to envelope us and invite us inside. A large old Swiss man came to the door and my human asked for a room. "We do not have one ready" he responded. My human stated that we would gladly wait and both of us were led inside.

Droplets of water fell from us both onto the floor as the remaining ice that clung to our coats quickly thawed in the welcoming warmth of the building. My human began taking off his outer clothing as a young girl bought him a coffee. I longed for something hot to drink but in public it would have been impolite for me to drink coffee from a cup! I could feel the warm air wrapping itself around my body. Still shivering uncontrollably, the warmth began making its way through to my bones.

Before long the girl summoned us both upstairs. Her English was very poor and she seemed reluctant to speak any German. She opened the door to a large room with two beds in it. A small table and a single chair stood in one corner and a tiny window gave a view of the snow-covered mountains behind. The timber floor was dusty and our damp footprints left a trail through the doorway. My human was not too impressed with the cleanliness of the room but it was relatively cheap, dry and warm so we were only too glad to take it. Beggars cannot be choosers and we were glad of anywhere that would protect us through the night.

As soon as the girl had gone, my human dried me with one of the spare blankets and placed me on top of the single bed. He then stripped off his damp clothing and laid a sleeping bag out on the double bed. Linen was provided but appeared dirty, a fact that was confirmed by the dead wasps that fell from one of the blankets. It appeared that the wasps had been trapped inside since last season and lay undisturbed eventually dehydrated and breaking into hundreds of pieces as they fell onto the floor.

We rested for a couple of hours before my human dressed himself and headed downstairs for some dinner. He left me in the room where I soon became frightened. As he sat downstairs, the girl went to him and as she signified tears rolling down her cheeks with her fingers she stated "Doggy go wah, wah, wah. Bring down". My human did as she told and to my delight she gave me a huge pork sausage. It was so large that I was not too sure how to eat it until my human had broken it into pieces. Until then I had sat on the floor dribbling with an eight inch sausage hanging from my mouth.

The old Swiss man sat with us as my human consumed a huge pile of liver and onions that the girl had prepared. "Is that your grand daughter?" asked my human. "No, she my wife" stated the Swiss man in broken English. "I sixty-two, she twenty-three. Good yes" he stated proudly. He then smiled as he followed this statement with "My wife she get old and fat so I divorce her and get new wife. I bring from Latvia. Was easy. Now she with me five year. She make old man very happy". My human politely nodded and continued eating. As the Swiss man left us, the girl returned to the room almost as though one of them had to keep an eye on us at all times.

The other rooms were occupied by Swiss school children on a curriculum enforced working holiday to prepare the Alps for summer. The inclement weather had forced them inside for the day where they had eventually grown bored of being inside with little to do. I became a source of interest and had to "endure" several pairs of hands stroking and petting me. After a while though they also grew tired of me and decided to return to their rooms. The girl was asking questions about me and about England but her English was very poor.

I listened with interest initially as I hoped that she would give me another sausage. Sadly this was not to be and I fell asleep with my head pressed against a hot radiator. As I drifted off to sleep, the tune of an old Desmond Dekker song began to play in my head. In my dream I found myself singing "Ooh ooh ohoh me ears are alight". Suddenly I woke up and shook my head vigorously. The heat from the radiator had burned my ear! My human noticed my discomfort and gave me some fuss. This was reassuring but I must admit that I was a little embarrassed especially as both he and the girl were laughing at me. After saying good night to the girl we climbed the stairs to bed and I watched as my human stuffed huge amounts of kitchen roll into his boots in an effort to dry them. We both snuggled into bed and slept very soundly.

Still Alive

DURING OUR crossing of Foo Pass the cold had stiffened my limbs. When I woke the next morning I spent a few minutes lying on my side, stretching my aching legs and wondering what state my pads were in whilst I yawned and yawned and yawned. The aches were a good ache, the sort you get after a hard workout; kind of satisfying and comfortable. I apprehensively rose to my feet. My pads tingled as they took my weight but I knew this feeling would soon subside. The tingling and stiffness would go away as exercise forced the circulation of my blood. It was good to feel the aches and pains as only a few hours before, I had assumed that Death had taken me into his arms.

Our timber clad room was warm and dry. The silence outside was overpowering punctuated only by the sound of cooking from downstairs. I could smell breakfast and I knew that the Latvian girl would want to feed me with meat. She was kind and whilst neither I nor my human could barely understand a word she said, we both knew that she liked dogs and would spoil me. I watched as my human dressed and then repacked the rucksack. He had stuffed screwed up kitchen roll into his boots to dry them internally. It appeared to have worked as they no longer squelched as he placed his foot inside though I dread to think how much paper he had used to dry them. Images of homeless squirrels began flooding into my head.

Looking from the window I could see that wet snow was still falling steadily but the covering had not increased during the night.

This would mean that we would leave the alp building and continue our journey. The cold and wet snow was somewhat foreboding but I knew that we needed to go on. My human would never be defeated by a mountain and neither would I. Mind you, I think both of us were certain that we had been very lucky the previous day and I am sure that hypothermia would have set in had it not been for the Swiss lothario and his nubile Latvian wife.

We said our goodbyes and strode off into the white landscape. The route ahead would be arduous and the weather looked likely to remain cold and wet. We had seen no forecasts but instinct suggested that until the wind changed direction, the wet weather would persist. Unfortunately mountainous regions tend to experience clouds getting stuck in the valleys and showing no sign of respite until they have rained themselves dry. My human was clad head to toe in Gore-Tex but I just had my wet fur coat, the stiff breeze cut through my fur and bit into my skin. My ears were stinging and my nose was frozen like a little black ice cube.

After passing Mittler Stafel, the way became easier. The snow was still falling but it was no longer sticking on the ground, choosing instead to thaw almost upon impact. A decent farm road had been constructed on a winding route through the forest. The trees creaked and groaned in the wind like the old lady's hairy knees, their needle covered branches encrusted in heavy wet snow. Every so often the snow would drop in big lumps to the ground and splat like a heavy wet cow pat next to me.

Icy cold streams tumbled and frothed down the hillside and through culverts under the road. I could feel the vibration of the torrents as I walked over the culverts and occasionally I had to paddle my way through water wherever the culverts were too small to take the capacity of water. Regularly the trees gave way to meadows full of long grass and flowers whose heads hung heavy under the weight of thawing snow. I imagined that all the plants wished they had maintained their winter slumber for a couple of weeks longer rather than having to endure this late cold snap that froze their leaves and delicate petals.

The gaps in the trees should have given way to views across the valley to the Tschingelhoren but instead all I could see through my single eye was the inside of the surrounding clouds which were far too cold and heavy to manage to float above the valley floor let alone to drift high above the snowy mountain peaks. This was an area frequented by chamois pursued by a dying breed of chamois hunters; I kept my eye peeled for a glimpse of the agile hairy beasts but none were to be found and neither were the elusive chamois. The sound of roaring waterfalls echoed all around but I could only imagine how beautiful their foaming waters would look as they glistened in the sunlight that we should have been enjoying in June.

My feet were still sore and despite the soreness being numbed by the cold, I longed to be wearing warm and dry Gore-Tex lined leather boots such as those my human was wearing. To have each step cushioned by a Vibram sole would be heavenly. Alas it was not to be but to my surprise, with the weather as bad as it was, we would be camping in Elm for the night. Yes, you did read that correctly. The farm road soon gave way to a public highway which led the way in long sweeping loops past the campsite and on into the attractive but straggling village of Elm.

Upon arrival at the campsite, my human tied my lead to a tree and left me sitting under its inadequate shelter alongside his rucksack. I huddled myself into a ball and watched as he proceeded to erect the tent. I knew it would be a long cold night under the nylon roof which whilst keeping us dry would still allow the cold damp air to penetrate my bones through my sodden coat. The comforts of central heating would be very welcome but a long time coming for we were not to sleep inside a building again for a fortnight.

The elderly campsite owner watched as the tent went up. I gathered from her expression that she could hardly believe neither the madness nor determination of my human to camp out in the weather we were enduring. When we went into her hut to pay for one nights stay, she commented that only the English would be stupid enough to spend a night outdoors in this weather. My human smiled and stated "But its summer". I think she understood but her face was still stuck with a puzzled expression upon it; I must admit that I knew exactly how she felt.

The day was still young and my human was hungry so we headed into Elm. It was a good opportunity for us to stock up on supplies at the local supermarket and bakery. The fresh cooked bread smelt heavenly as I stood outside the doorway and I almost ate its warm aroma. The houses, including the Suworowhaus named after a Russian general who had stayed there following a series of defeats at the hands of Napoleons soldiers, were neatly decked out in colourful flowers whose vivid red blooms brightly stood out against the white walls and even whiter snow. I longed to see the sun shine through St Martin's Hole and illuminate the church tower as it does on just two days of the year but the sun was to stay firmly hidden just like Piz Sardona and Piz Segnas which would normally provide a stunning backdrop to the same 15th Century church.

This was a village that had quietly endured its own 9-11 tragedy when in 1881 the 500m Plattenbergkopf had collapsed killing 114 people. However, here there is no Ground Zero; the meadows show no sign of the turmoil that they must have witnessed. As we headed back to the tent, I hoped that I would not observe such a rock fall.

The snow was still steadily falling as we entered the tent whose roof now hung heavy under a layer of white flakes. My human used paper towels from the campsite toilets to dry me as we got into the tent. He hung his wet Gore-Tex in the small porch and zipped us both into the inner tent. He then placed my ration of biscuits into my bowl and proceeded to eat the food he had purchased in the village. His smoked sausage and pastries smelt far better than my boring biscuits so I watched intently in the hope that I may be given a morsel. Frustratingly my portion turned out to be less than a square inch of pastry though I did get a fair share of the fresh milk. The milk was cold but very nourishing and made a refreshing change to the iced water I had been drinking for the past couple of days.

It was still light as my human zipped himself into his down filled sleeping bag. I snuggled against his feet and as I drifted into a deep slumber, I listened to the pattering of snow falling on the tent then whooshing in clumps down the walls. Occasionally I would feebly growl to warn off any passing animals that may be disturbing our frosting of snow. I was fairly sure that the snows movement was the result of gravity but as we were sleeping out in the wilderness of the Swiss Alps, I knew it was my duty to guard my human. In reality I was too tired to offer any sort of defence against attacking beasts but I felt better for having made some sort of effort. I just hoped that the snow would ease before dawn as another cold and wet walk was far from appealing. I also wished that my human would stop snoring!

Elm

BY MORNING my fur was still damp from the previous days drenching and only my own body warmth had prevented my fur from freezing. A frosting of ice lined the inside of our tent where rising moisture had condensed on the roof of the inner tent. During the night my constant shivering and the whooshing noise created by the layers of snow sliding off the tents fabric had disturbed any chance of sleep. My bones ached and my eye lid was heavy. I needed the toilet but could not be bothered to unfurl my body and head outside into the cold and wet dawn air.

My human was also awake but like me, he lay silent and still but unlike me he was in a nice warm sleeping bag. As the wind gusted, snow could be heard brushing against the outside of the tent. The temperature had dropped significantly during the night and would make the going tough during the day ahead. It was a day that I was far from enthralled about and looked upon with an element of dread. We had travelled to walk in the early summer sun, not the late winter snows.

The alarm had sounded at seven o'clock but it would be more than thirty minutes before my human plucked up the courage to extract himself from his Kimmlite bag and venture out into the 'winter' wonderland. As I stepped outside, my feet sank a couple of inches into the soft snow. I looked up towards the surrounding peaks but they were nowhere to be seen. Even the steeple of the church in nearby Elm seemed to penetrate the low slung clouds as they hurried along in the strengthening easterly winds. If only the winds had turned to come from the South bringing the Mediterranean warmth with them, things would be so different. Alas that was not to be, least not for a few more days.

Having washed himself and prepared his rucksack, my human began taking the tent down. For this procedure to work effectively I needed to stay out of the tent. There were no other campers but then I would not expect there to be any. The weather was decidedly inclement and as the owner had stated, only mad dogs and Englishmen would ever venture out in such conditions. In fact the prospect of crossing not one but two mountain passes sent even bigger shivers down my spine but we were to push on. Thankfully odd glimpses of blue sky could be seen through tiny breaks in the cloud but the Sun was certainly hiding. As we had the site to ourselves, I was allowed to wander off my lead. My human knew I would not stray too far and laughed at me when I huddled under a nearby conifer for what little shelter it provided.

I watched as he brushed the heavy snow from the tent and first un-pegged prior to tying up the guide ropes. He then allowed the tent to collapse in a controlled manner onto the grounds and knelt in the snow to roll the tent up and pack it tightly into its bag. The bag was then wrapped in a polythene sack and strapped securely into his rucksack which he lifted onto his back before proceeding towards the village of Elm. I continued to watch as he walked away. I tried hard to will him to stay, to stop walking and put the tent back up. Or better still, to check us both into a nice warm hotel. Fairly soon I had to crawl out from under the conifer and run through the snow to catch my human. Had I waited much longer he would have disappeared into the mist.

Elm was only a brief walk away and it was there that my human paused to buy some pain au chocolat and milk which he consumed for breakfast. Thankfully I was given a few morsels and thoroughly enjoyed lapping up the creamy milk.

Maybe my human was not that mad after all; the breaks in the cloud had increased in size and frequency. The temperature had risen by a few degrees and the snow that coated the ground was rapidly thawing. Water dripped from the rooftops and tumbled down the copper rainwater pipes before it trickled over the tarmac and cobbles. Maybe, just maybe, we might get a whole day that would remain clear.

As we exited the village, the surrounding meadows were full of flowers and lush grasses which stood in silence. The weather had given the plants a last minute reprieve as the cows were confined to their sheds rather than munching the lush greenery to a chorus of ringing bells.

Suddenly things seemed to take an even better turn. My human had decided to ease the days walk by taking the minibus to Ober Erbs. This bus ride would save two hours walking and provide more time for the clouds to clear and the rain and sleet to ease. Embarrassingly it was here that I made a complete prat of myself. Normally I am a bright and intelligent dog but this was, as you will no doubt remember, only my second ever bus ride.

When we boarded the first bus, my human had just walked through the open doors and we had sat roughly midway along the vehicle. This time the bus was far smaller and my human appeared to be turned away by the driver. However, as I was behind my human and still standing on the pavement, I could not tell exactly what was happening. We walked along the side of the bus and my human opened a small door low on the side of the bus. He them proceeded to remove his rucksack and push it through the small door. Due to the size of his rucksack, he appeared to struggle so I thought it a good idea to save a bit of time and using my initiative I jumped on board and headed to the far side of the tiny room.

My human failed to notice that I had boarded until I had reached the far side of the bus and lay snuggled within the other passengers' luggage. I became confused as my human called me back and rather than obediently respond to his call, I stay put. Eventually he crawled inside, "at last!" I thought "he has finally decided to crawl in a lay with me" but then he just grabbed my lead and as he reversed out backwards, he pulled me with him and back out into the cold and wet street. I was reluctantly pulled along the paving slabs. Why were we leaving the rucksack in the warm bus? As my human led me up the steps at the front of the bus it suddenly dawned on me. What I had presumed to be the seating area for people with dogs was actually the luggage hold! I felt very stupid and lay embarrassed on the floor as the bus began its journey along the rough cobbles and up the winding road from the railway station to Ober Erbs.

At the head of the road we alighted from the bus. I blushed as my human retrieved his rucksack. Looking around from our vantage point at 1,710m, I could see the glaciers of the Haustock glistening in fleeting moments of sunlight. Vivid splashes of blue sky lifted my spirits and the surrounding mountains were a real picture standing tall above the valley floor, their lower slopes lush and green with a frosting of fresh white snow from the waist up. Patches of mist and cloud rose from the trees and headed up towards the sky. The warmth of the sun gave a very welcome respite from the cold we had previously endured and as we walked from the road to head along a stony track, steam rose before our feet.

Sadly upon reaching a signpost, the stony track gave way to a path following red and white bergweg markers. The path had been churned by cattle and I was literally chest high in thick wet mud and cow pats. My pure white legs were black with the rancid sludge but at least it was warm! The path led to a pastureland bowl and crossed several roaring streams en-route. The icy streams washed the mud and manure from my legs before they quickly became thickly encrusted time and again.

My legs would finally be washed clean five minutes from the bowl as I had to swim the main stream at the head of the valley. I hate swimming and this was the second time on this trip that I had been forced to swim a stream. The waters were even colder this time and once again I was tied to my human though on this occasion the velocity of the stream was more manageable. Even so, I was far happier when we had reached the other side and I was able to run free. However, I was unable to dry the icy water from my coat as the lush meadow grasses in the area were still thickly coated in wet snow.

A snow covered zigzag path headed up a grassy spur to the southwest. As we followed it, my human slipped several times on the glassy ice-coated rocks that lay hidden in the snow. It was a slow climb and tiring for a dog whose strength and body warmth had already been sapped by cold glacial waters. Pretty soon we were contouring the hillside to a saddle near the Erbser Stock. We were at a height of around 2,150m and well above the snow line. Soft wet snow had given way to firm crisp snows that I could walk on without falling through the surface. My sodden fur was penetrated by biting icy gusts of wind. As I looked back, I could see the route we had used to descend the Foo Pass in such atrocious conditions just two days previous. I wondered how the Latvian girl who had fed me warm sausages was doing and wished that she might suddenly appear with a huge bratwurst with my name upon it! My mouth watered at the mere thought and my stomach rumbled.

The Richetlipass lay ahead with dark clouds threateningly descending its rocky flanks. Whilst we had so far proceeded in improving conditions, the clouds ahead were far more foreboding. Descending in long loops towards the lonely building of

Wichlenmatt at 2,037m I hung my head and tail low. The building sat in remote solitude amidst the beckoning silence of a true mountain wilderness. Firm snow still lay around us but on this side of the pass the size and frequency of the larger patches had reduced significantly. Lush green flower strewn meadows had given way to windswept brown grass as we followed our route down. I could see that the downhill would soon give way to an arduous ascent. Buzzards circled silently overhead like vultures and made me stick close to my human lest they swooped for a quick snack on a terrier. Okay, so they may not be partial to dog, but what if they were really hungry?

As we descended into the deep valley of the Durnachtal I kept my eye open for anymore hungry looking birds but not for long as the descent was steep on a narrow winding path which was incredibly slippery in the wet snow. I was very pleased to reach a small hut on a spur. Not only did it give me some much needed shelter for a few minutes whilst my human took some refreshments but it also signified the start of a far more stable path. The snow was still falling around us but the new path was far more prominent making our onward journey slightly more pleasant as we walked along a moraine crest.

My relief at reaching the moraine crest was sadly short lived for at the end of the crest our descent steepened significantly. I hate going downhill as it hurts my front paws as I struggle to stop my legs running away from me. It was particularly difficult here in the snow which in places had turned to ice. In one section my human had to hold onto ice encrusted fixed chains that were so cold his glove actually stuck to the chains. I was glad I did not have to hold onto the chains particularly as I do not have any hands but also because my full concentration and effort was being used to maintain grip on the stony ground that was covered in patches of black ice. After every few paces I would slip forward in a gravity assisted descent. With every slip I gained momentum momentarily and each time that happened my bum tightened as my heart skipped a beat or two. I had just one thought in mind; gravity kills me. I dug my claws into the ice with all my might and continued downhill. A wooden bridge lay at the foot of the valley and ensured that my frozen paws did not have to enter the icy stream though I had to take extreme care when negotiating the gaps in the timber slats.

A footpath signposted to Linthal Bachweg looked to give a more interesting route to Linthal but due to the worsening weather my human decided to follow the paved road in order to speed our progress to a safe nights sleep rather than negotiate yet more icy rocks.

We camped just outside of Linthal; a pleasant but sprawling village which is in fact the highest village in the valley. The village sits at the end of a branch line on the Zurich to Chur railway. I longed to board one of the warm and comfortable trains. My night was a restless one as I felt the temperature dropping rapidly. My human was also restless due to the cold. We spent the entire night huddled together shivering and dozing whenever we could. By morning my wet fur had become encrusted with frost and we were both awake at first light. Or perhaps it was second light; I could not work out whether I may have slept through the first.

Altdorf

FTER A very bad nights sleep I awoke with a covering of ice on my fur. The temperature had dropped significantly during the night and was still well below freezing. It was snowing hard and gritty snow which made it sound as though the tent was being sand blasted by every gust of wind. As we emerged from the tent it became obvious that a difficult day lay ahead. A day that would start with my human having to remove a snow drift from the side of the tent. The water that had remained in my bowl and drinking bottle overnight had frozen solid. I wanted to drink but dare not lick the ice lest my tongue stuck to it!

The snow had stopped falling but the small flakes were being blown around in the stiff breeze. I sheltered near some rocks as my human took the tent down and packed it away. He neglected to take a drink or to eat in order that the tent could be packed away and we could make our way towards Altdorf and hopefully get warmed up.

Very soon we were at the base station of the funicular to Braunwald. Signs there indicated that the Klausenpass was closed to vehicles due to the heavy snowfall. We would have to walk the entire distance to Altdorf rather than take a postbus at any point.

The funicular was warm and snug. I stood in the front car with my human. All I could see was the timber floor and walls. The floor was wet with melted snow and a soft warmth rose through the wood, its varnished surface worn by hundreds of shoes and boots. In here we were protected from the biting wind which would soon take my breath away as we alighted at the summit station into Braunwald from where we would negotiate a very cold balcony path.

The weather was clearer though it was still bitterly cold and low clouds hurried their way along the valley brushing the hillsides as they went. The Tödi stood at the head of the valley proudly living up to its name as the "King of the Little Mountains". Its craggy rocks encrusted in bright white snow. The Urner Boden is a unique Swiss valley which strongly resembles Norway. Clouds obscured much of the valley but through the frequent breaks I could see a long expanse of pasture with small herdsmen's huts and dairy farms scattered over its floor. Still there was no clanging of cow bells as all the cows were safely tucked up in soft warm hay in the barns below us. I would have loved to snuggle into some warm soft hay but it was not to be. For me it would be a long day, struggling against the biting cold and the constant heavy snow showers. The temperature had risen slightly but this merely meant that the snow flakes grew in size and increased in wetness.

As we walked along the edge of a forest I was glad of the shelter the trees afforded us. They offered protection from the biting wind but not from the clumps of snow that fell from the pine tree branches. I was soaked! My fur was drenched and had taken on a slightly spiky appearance and I had a frosting of snow on top of my nose. The path soon contoured towards Hinter Stafel before descending steeply to the Klausen road and the canton boundary. Crossing a pass or a boundary made Montreux seem far closer but I knew we still had several days to go before we would reach the banks of Lake Geneva.

The snow was still falling and our path was well hidden below its surface. No traffic was to be seen on the snow covered tarmac road so my human decided we should follow it. This normally bustling section of road belonged to us today, our six feet providing the only evidence of life on the surface of the road. Bergweg paths crossed the road but their red and white painted markers were completely hidden below the surface of the snow. A small herd of chamois silently watched our progress from their vantage point a few hundred feet above us. I could not work out whether they were worried by us or bemused by our madness at being out in such conditions. Under normal circumstances we should be snuggled up in a centrally heated house looking out across the picturesque snow covered mountains not trudging through deepening snow.

The summit of the Klausenpass gave us a panoramic view of the inside of a big grey cloud! All that effort wasted as we could have just as easily been in the English Fens as on a Swiss mountain. This route had been used for centuries to connect Uri and Glarus and was one of the first to see motorised traffic but not today; my human and I stood alone listening to the sound of silence on the summit of the pass. The refreshment kiosk was closed and the tiny chapel was all but hidden in the thick mist.

Before the intense cold managed to get a grip on us, we began our long descent towards Altdorf, the home of William Tell. I hoped that my human would not decide to put an apple on my head and shoot it off for I felt certain he would miss!

Our descent from the 1,948m Klausenpass to the village of Äsch would be swift; part walking, part slipping and part running. The sight of the tremendously spectacular Stäubifall was a welcome interlude to our descent. Its roaring waters drowned out any chance of hearing any other noises. The continual rain, sleet and snow we had endured for the past few days cascaded ninety metres over a craggy cliff sending up a massive plume of spray and vibrating the ground beneath my feet. I watched part in awe and part in fear as I wondered at the ferocity of the waters.

We crossed the stream that runs from the Stäubifall and came to the second part of the hamlet of Äsch which consists of just a few chalets and a tiny chapel where we would take much needed shelter whilst my human shared his lunch with me. I sat shivering in front of him as he sat on a wooden bench within the tiny chapel. Melting snow trickled down my humans clothing and onto his seat from where it fell and created tiny pools on the floor. Puddles also formed around his feet and the water from my fur formed a puddle around me. Had the water not been clear, you would have sworn I had had an accident. Truth was I was so cold that the contents of my bladder were quite possibly frozen within me!

The chapel smelt fusty and its walls were old and tired. A good coat of paint would not have gone amiss but the poor décor merely served to enhance our surroundings. There was no heating but the fact that it was no longer snowing on us and that we were protected from the chilled wind meant that it felt warm. Above the fusty smell of the chapel, the aroma of my humans smoked sausage filled the air tempting my mouth to water as I waited for my share. I greedily ate all I was given but I am certain that no matter how much food my human had donated to me that day, it would never have been enough. The physical effort required to cross our coldest pass to date was incredible but still paled in comparison to the crossing of Foo Pass just a few days earlier.

Whilst we sheltered, the air had warmed and the snow fall turned to rain. The rain drops fell heavily and pounded on the chapel roof. A constant drip, drip, drip echoed within the four walls as water fell through a hole in the chapel roof. My human wandered around the church reading inscriptions on the walls and alter. There was quite a lot of writing on big slabs on the floor. At first I was sickened at the thought of walking on dead people but then a thought hit me; under those slabs there would be bones! Big juicy marrow filled thigh bones. My mouth watered at the thought but then the more I thought about it, the more off putting the images became. Smelly and mouldering human bones certainly would not be as nice as a juicy smoked sausage.

All too soon my human was doing up his jacket and putting his rucksack back on. I said my goodbyes to the spirits. I knew I was not really allowed to enter a church because dogs do not have souls. I do though as I have my four boots so I actually have four soles but they were in my humans' rucksack so I was not sure whether they counted as they were not on my feet.

The rain was heavy and horizontal in the wind. I tucked my ears and head down and squinted my eye as we walked into the wind. I was soon soaked through again; the water even seeped under my collar wetting my neck!

We continued our descent towards Altdorf partly on the deserted road and partly on narrow stony paths. Occasional patches of blue sky gave hope of some summer warmth but the hope was short lived. No sooner had the warm rays of the sun hit my fur than they were gone, hidden behind a shroud of mist which was thousands of feet thick.

I plodded a rhythmic walk as we entered Burglen, the birth place of William Tell and home to the famous Tell Museum. As we crossed the main road from the museum to the chapel that is built on the site of the house in which Tell was born, I looked nervously at a fruit stall outside a small shop. A chubby Swiss girl was restocking the stall but thankfully she was placing oranges upon it; there were no apples to be seen. Phew! I would not have to suffer the indignity of being photographed with a Bramley strapped to my head!

Our stop in Burglen was brief, just long enough for my human to take a couple of photographs and then we headed on the final leg to Altdorf. Initially our route crossed a river and then we entered a narrow and dark road tunnel. Water was dripping through the roof and trickling down the tarmac as we walked up a relatively steep gradient. I wondered just how long this tunnel was as I could see no light at the end of it. I could however hear ghostly voices. A shudder ran down my spine as the hairs of my hackles stood up. The spirits in the chapel of Äsch had been friendly and inviting but this place appeared more sinister.

We dogs are finely tuned to connect with the spirit world. When our hackles stand up it is usually because a ghost is nearby. When we growl for no reason, suddenly standing alert and staring at what humans think is an empty space; we are actually protecting our humans from a troubled soul, warning it to return to its wanderings within the netherland between heaven and hell. Oblivious to this our humans usually tell us to lie down and be quiet. If only they knew.

I was still on my lead as I had been since we had departed Burglen. I pulled ahead, my eye and all my senses straining to see the ghostly spectre that lay ahead. As we reached a sharp bend in the tunnel, I realised that a chapel had been carved within the tunnel. Lighted candles illuminated a small alter with a gold coloured cross standing upon it and flowers arranged in vases. Then I saw it; a dishevelled old lady, the olive skin of her face deeply wrinkled. She stared at us and smiled like a Sun Maid raisin with eyes and grey hair swept back under a dark coloured head scarf. Her mouth was open slightly and three yellow and brown teeth hung loosely from her top jaw. A bite from those would be very nasty. I nervously continued towards her and noticed that her stocking clad legs were far hairier than mine but this was no ghostly spectre, this was a real walking, talking old lady. She greeted us both and proceeded to kneel down and pray. My human stopped again for a photograph but we did not loiter. We needed to get to Altdorf and I think my human was nervous in case the old lady might think she had pulled!

As we walked towards the light at the end of the tunnel, I became conscious of light footsteps behind us. A young girl of around fourteen years joined us. She smiled at me and stroked my head as we walked. She told my human that her name was Izzy. The braces on her teeth flickered as she spoke, reflecting what little light was entering the tunnel. Izzy was a friendly girl on her way home from school and enjoyed her half English and half German conversation with my human as we walked from the tunnel. At a sharp hairpin bend, Izzy said her auf weidersehns before turning sharp right as we continued ahead on a stone covered track. Piles of timber stood precariously along the side of the track and Izzy waved to us as she disappeared around a corner.

In what seemed like just a few minutes, we were entering Altdorf near to some poorly maintained tennis courts and there before us was the huge bronze statue of William Tell in Rathausplatz. The town was a noisy place full of bustling tourists all eager for a photograph of William Tell on the site of the point where he allegedly shot the apple from his son's head. Despite a great fire in 1799 and the narrow traffic filled main street, the town maintains a certain amount of character.

It was still raining heavily as we entered the campsite. Watched by a small group of German motorcyclists, my human erected our tent and we snuggled inside. The dampness in the air and within our kit was ever present. Neither of us could get warm as my human cooked his dinner and fed me my biscuits. I longed for a roaring open fire; a massive one in a huge stone fireplace with whole oak trees burning on it and sending enormous flames up into the chimney as a hog slowly roasted on a revolving spit. Sadly my dream could not come to fruition but the thoughts did warm me psychologically and kept me going through the night.

From the moment we entered our tent at six in the evening, we stayed until morning. Both of us dozed as much as possible but occasionally unable to even hear above the noise of the wind and rain outside. The constant pounding on the tent was tortuous and only served to heighten the sensation of the cold and damp air. The night was a long one but by morning the rain was still falling. The walk ahead to Engleberg would be a long slog over our fourth pass; if only I could have lived with a normal human who would take me on a Devonshire beach holiday or even just leave me in the kennels. My feet were sore and so wet that they were threatening to become webbed. In fact I felt certain I must be an amphibious dog as I had remained wet through since we had left Liechtenstein. I swore he would regret it if I was to come down with trench paw!

In the footsteps of Holmes

THE NIGHT passed without incident but when I awoke it was still bitterly cold and I was still damp which would mean lots of worries about trench paw. Yes us dogs do have 'four wheel drive' but that also means we have twice as many sore feet as you humans and trench paw would be a serious concern with all this wet weather and the cold.

As the tent came down, so did the rain and the clouds were also hanging as low as a daschunds bits. The cloud was the biggest shame as the walk from Altdorf to Engleberg has been described as one of the nicest stages of the Alpine Pass Route with a clearly defined trail and amazing views along every step of the way. Yet we were destined to be shrouded in mist.

Following an aromatic stop at the local bakers, we set off. The temperature was not rising and the picturesque dusting of snow on the surrounding mountains seemed to be creeping ever lower. We were to start the day at 447m and rise to the summit of the Surenenpass at 2,291m just prior to the half way point. However, due to the weather, my human decided it would be prudent to take the local bus to Attinghausen and then the cable car to Brüsti. This was a decision for which I was incredibly grateful as it would avoid the initial road walk and a steep uphill trek to Brüsti through forest. Forest is great when it is downhill or flat as it is full of other animals; squirrels, deer, bears, wolves, lions…Okay so maybe some of those animals are not resident in the wilds of Switzerland but they do have them in Zurich zoo and I have watched Madagascar; I know they can escape. It would be a foolish dog indeed that did not go prepared and plan for the worst case scenario.

We waited momentarily at the bus stop and with legendary Swiss precision, the bus arrived as the town clock struck eight o'clock and, unlike in England, this did not signal the arrival of the 07.15 bus! Inside was warm and cramped. The rubber floors were wet from countless feet before mine and the stench of diesel filled the air but it was warm and sheltered us from the wind. The bus grunted and groaned its way out of the early morning Altdorf traffic and on towards Attinghausen with the elderly driver crunching his way into whatever gear the wayward gearlever selected. I could see that we were not missing much of a walk as the path we should have taken passed below the railway lines and motorway before following the river upstream. Plumes of spray pirouetted behind speeding cars on the motorway all but obscuring their polluting presence. In a brief burst of sunlight a small rainbow appeared in the spray above the tarmac only to disappear as a car sped through without stopping to admire its vivid colours. Had the driver even noticed? I very much doubt it.

Attinghausen itself is unimpressive. Historically important as the birthplace of Walter Fürst, it now forms a characterless commuter village and is massively overshadowed by its neighbour, Altdorf.

Other than a few school children, the village was quiet as we passed though and boarded the cable car up to Brüsti. The cable car was a battered old thing; its paintwork flaking and its Perspex windows were scarred by years of abuse and yellowing with age. I could barely see out as we rattled and creaked our way uphill and through the clouds.

By the time we had passed though the initial cloud layer and arrived in Brüsti, occasional glimpses of Lake Lucerne or the

Vierwaldstättersee as it is really called were visible. However, it was the iced summit of the Titlis that really grabbed my attention. Even on a grey and murky day, it stood as a proud and impressive focal point that would accompany us down into Engelberg.

The final hours walk to the pass initially follows a long, and if you have bare feet, painful scree slope. I was taking four paw steps forward and three back as we ascended. Each slip seemed to take a layer of skin off my pads which were by now almost glowing due to the friction. However, we were soon crossing snow fields before ascending very steep zigzags to the summit of the pass. It had taken two and a half long hours to reach the summit of the pass but with almost perfect timing, the bulk of the cloud had cleared offering a wondrous view across the Titlis whose shoulder we were due to cross tomorrow.

Below us stood the Seewen Tarns, trapped within snow covered pasture with their frozen waters shining turquoise through a thin layer of crisp fresh snow. The scene was straight from a Christmas card but this was early June, the time when normally one should be picnicking beside the tarns, not avoiding stepping on their icy covering.

We descended from the pass through snow covered pastures deserted by the sheep that normally graze the grasses. Just past Alphütte Blackenalp, the babbling waterfall fell across ice covered rocks with icicles steadily growing in the spray like huge organ pipes.

Eventually we reached our first major mountain resort of the Swiss Alpine Pass Route, Engelberg. The town developed around a huge Benedictine monastery which was founded early in the twelfth century. Our arrival in the town was a major relief to a tired, sore and aching Smooth Fox Terrier at the end of a day that had seen our calmest weather to date and prior to one which would see us arrive in Meiringen, the home of the meringue and the town that was made famous by the death of Sherlock Holmes. The campsite, which is open all year, was excellent and offered a sheltered place to stay for the night.

Following a refreshingly calm night, we set off for Meiringen. It would be another long day but would be slightly easier as our height gain would be less than previous days.

My human knew that my feet were sore as I had reluctantly roused myself from my bed and very tentatively walked across the campsite. My legs were almost as stiff as those of a dead dog and my paws throbbed with every step. Even the tiniest piece of grit seemed to dig deep into my pads. I tried desperately to avoid putting my full weight down on my feet but that was physically impossible and I made a plethora of silent yelps, groans and curses as we started off. Thankfully before long my pain eased; not because anything was hurting less but because my feet became numb as the muscles in my legs loosened. In order to save my feet and to ensure that we made it to Meiringen, my human decided we would make full use of the gondolas and cableways to the Jochpass.

The huge quantity of metalwork lining our route did detract somewhat from the beauty of the surrounding mountains but my feet felt so much better for its presence. Quietly drifting above the rough track was far more satisfying than walking along it. As I jumped from the final gondola, I felt a reluctance to proceed the remainder of our day's route but as we descended to the Engstlensee and left the cableways behind, the Wetterhorn rose ahead of us like a huge meringue and I wondered if this was how the Meiringers came up with the idea for their culinary invention.

Much of the descent into Meiringen was on very steep loose surfaces and it was on these that my pads finally gave way. The numbness I had so far felt turned into a sharp and excruciating pain as the sore red patches on my feet turned first to blisters and then to raw patches. My human soon noticed that I was lagging behind and that I had blood splashing onto my white fur.

This was an increasingly familiar experience for both of us and we were now well prepared. In an undignified manner, my human rolled me onto my back, sprayed my sore paws with Savlon and then placed my boots onto my two front feet. For some reason my front feet always wear out prior to my hind feet.

The remainder of the day was spent with me trying to avoid people. Whenever anyone sees me with my boots on, they point and stare as if they have never seen a dog wearing boots. If dogs did not wear boots then stores would not sell them. In any case, cats wear them all the time; look at Puss in Boots!

The campsite in Meiringen was a tip. The ground was covered in loose stones, it was slightly flooded and trees overhung all round. My human found the clearest area and got our tent up just before the rain returned. The heavy rain and snow we had endured over previous days had returned with a vengeance. We took shelter inside and listened to the constant hammering of rain on the tent, the crashing of the nearby waterfalls and the Swiss Air Force jets taking off and landing at the nearby military base. Noises do not scare me, I even attend firework displays, but with all this going on, sleep was nigh on impossible. Then there was the relentless shivering. The temperature had dropped significantly very quickly and the dampness in the air chilled me to the bone.

The ground within the campsite was already waterlogged and this rain was merely adding to it. The night was cold and miserable and seemed longer than ever. I barely slept a wink and next day the rain was still coming down. However, the rain was falling as snow only five hundred metres above us which would make it impossible to cross the Grosse Scheidegg which at 1,962m was some 1,400m above Meiringen. In fact it actually transpired that the Grosse Scheidegg was closed due to the heavy snowfall. All this resulted in my human deciding to stay at our waterlogged camp-site for an extra night and to explore Meiringen.

The town was weird. Everything around it related to Sherlock Holmes who had fictitiously met his death at the hands of Moriarty above the Reichenbach Falls. Lying at the head of an enormous u-shaped valley, Meiringen had been adopted by Victorian travellers from England and now shamelessly exploits its connection with the detective; Transport for London signs abound along with red telephone kiosks and even a Baker Street.

My human took me into the local tourist office where one of the girls asked if he would be willing to complete a quick survey. She was amazed when she asked "How did you travel to Meiringen?" My human answered "We walked." The girl questioned his answer as she had no box to tick for such a response. When my human explained where we had walked from and where we were heading to, she said that he must be mad but very fit. "Hello" I thought, "I'm down here!" It took her a while to realise that I was standing beside my human and that my four little legs had walked the same distance. I think she was too shocked to ask anymore questions and she just gave up. However, she did advise my human that the pass was likely to remain closed for a few more days.

My human was prepared to stay here for one day but anything more would be too much. Not because Meiringen was not a nice town but because the campsite was the worst we had ever stayed at outside of Italy. The old lady running it was miserable and did not like dogs. Mind you, I did not like her. The noise had driven us both mad the previous night and we knew there would be more of the same.

As most places were closed at the time of our visit, my human decided to eat at the local hospital. He had roast chicken and saved me the succulent skin. It was a pleasant surprise and I thoroughly enjoyed eating it and then being fed the same by two local nurses. I looked very pitiful and shivered as much as I could in order to attract their attention. It worked to perfection and I got some fuss too. In fact I think if I had stayed all day, I could have got the equivalent of an entire chicken but my human had other ideas.

We returned to the tent so that he could re-plan our route. After a couple of hours examining the maps to the constant roar of the waterfall, the incessant pounding of the rain and the roars of Swiss jets, a solution had been planned. We would walk along the valley to Brienz, then along the banks of Brienzer See prior to taking a paddle steamer to Interlaaken where I had visited the previous Christmas and finally camping for a night or two in Lauterbrunnen. It would mean missing the Grosse Scheidegg and Kleine Scheidegg but we had already walked both of those back in December when, despite the mid-winter snows, the temperature had seemed far more acceptable.

Both of us were damp as we settled down to sleep. It was only 7pm but with the constant heavy rain and the biting cold, it seemed the only sensible thing to do. My human fell straight into a deep sleep but his snores merely added to my discomfort. Occasionally he would wake as falling rocks tumbled and crashed down the waterfall loosened by the extreme snow and rainfall. I think we would both have felt happier if we had been able to move to a different campsite but alas that was not possible. All we could do was sit tight and hope that the rain would ease by morning. My feet were still sore but the short walk in Meiringen and long day and night in the tent would undoubtedly assist the healing process. I drifted to sleep shortly after counting my fifteen thousand and ninety-third sheep.

Diversion

THE NOISE during the night did not abate. Constant pouring rain pounded against the thin fabric of the tent, rocks tumbled and crashed their way down the nearby waterfall which roared loudly in the background. Water trickled through the ground all around us and my human snored. How on Earth was I meant to sleep through all that?

Daylight gradually crept over us. The valley was steeply u-shaped so there would have been no chance of a sun rise even if the cloud had cleared. No sudden warmth from the sun as it crept over the horizon and illuminated the tent with its vibrant rays. Instead a dull light crept over us but the temperature remained low.

My human was not stirring but I needed a wee. I held it for as long as I could but then I knew I was fighting a losing battle. I stirred from my position near his feet and walked up the length of his sleeping bag. With every step I stood my full weight on every part of his anatomy and then I reached the hole at the top of the bag. His eyes were open as I stood on his chest looking down into his face. My tail wagged wildly as I pricked my ears and looked excitedly into his sleepy eyes. He was not moving quite fast enough so I shoved my cold wet nose into his face and snorted a fine mist from my nose over his face. This always worked wonders! Before I knew it he was struggling to release his arms from within the sleeping bag and then wiping my saliva from his face.

He pushed me off his sleeping bag and asked if I wanted to go outside. Of course I did so I wagged my tail with greater vigour and pushed my head against the door of the tent. "Hang on" he said as he pulled me back. I had been too eager and was blocking his access to the zip. The instant the door was open far enough I squeezed through, ran to the nearest tree and lifted my leg high as I relieved myself. I felt so much better as I returned to the tent but now I was banned from entering because my feet were too wet. No, not because I had missed the tree and hit my feet but because the ground was waterlogged.

My human soon joined me outside and was pleasantly surprised to discover that the water falling on the tent was not rain but water dripping from the over hanging trees. The heavy rain had stopped and blue sky was visible through the low layer of cloud which hung just a few hundred feet above the valley floor.

My human quickly had the tent down and packed the wet fabric into his rucksack. He was eager to get going as the sun was now peering over the eastern mountain peaks and warming us with warmth we had not so far experienced on this trip.

The route to Brienz was reasonably flat. We soon set off at a brisk pace. My legs were still aching but my pads had healed and the warm sunshine added an extra spring to my step. The mountain sides were still white with thick snow. We had been lucky with the rain fall, as if we had been just five hundred feet higher, we would have been above the snow line and walking would have been so much more difficult. My human knew that Grosse Scheidegg would still be closed as the girl in the tourist office had stated it would take a couple of days to open or "zwei tag". Yes already my German was improving and I was quickly beginning to think of myself as a kleine Schweizer hunde.

Pretty soon we were away from the main road that runs through the valley and had joined a minor forest road with the railway line running alongside us. The track soon became forested and as we walked, steam rose steadily from the sodden undergrowth encouraged by the heat of the sun.

An old lady was unloading buckets from her car and carrying them to the ponds that lined our new route. She saw me walking towards her and bent down to greet me by stroking my head. She spoke to me softly in German. I think she was saying nice things but I could not understand a word of it! She then spoke to my human but quickly realised that he was English and that her German was beyond the realms of his understanding. Basic stuff was okay but she was trying to explain what was in the buckets. She showed him they were full of tadpoles and wanted to know what they were called in English as the German translates precisely to "horse's nails". She was very happy to learn their English name and as she walked away from us she repeated "tadpoles" over and over.

Suddenly a massive roar filled the air and the ground vibrated under my feet. I quickly trotted to my human's side and looked to the source of the noise. A Swiss Air Force jet was landing just a hundred feet from us, its red parachute slowing it quickly to a halt shortly before the end of the runway. No sooner had it taxied off the runway than another came down, then another and another. The air and quickly the ground were surrounded by dozens of khaki coloured planes that arrived like an invading force. We stood and watched as they all landed one after the other. I was fascinated by the sounds and the smell of the unburned fuel which filled the air.

As our air display came to an end, we continued towards Brienz. I wondered what it would have been like in Switzerland during the war and what was hidden in the surrounding mountains. Railway lines criss-crossed our path and disappeared through large grey steel doors into huge man-made caverns. It was impossible to see what was inside but at some point these now rusted rails must have carried considerable amounts of military hardware into their ingenious hiding places in the mountains. I desperately wanted to explore but there was no way in.

We soon walked underneath the motorway and up a hill which lead into a preserved rural Swiss village. Old houses and farmsteads surrounded us with donkeys, chickens, geese, goats and cows all around. One smell after another created the constant desire to chase another animal. Not to eat of course but to play with! Small groups of tourists were also walking around the village and, like my human, were photographing the unusual buildings. Whilst some followed the traditional Swiss chalet design, others took on an almost English Tudor appearance.

Our path twisted and turned its way through the ancient village and down a hillside into a modern town with small patches of grass being grazed by cows. Today we had met our first cows in several days their bells were ringing merrily as the chewed the cud. The snow on the surrounding hills was receding upwards and the sun was still shining brightly. My human was breaking into a sweat as the shimmering waters of the Brienzer See came into sight, its blue waters glistening with a silvery hue.

After a short walk through lush meadows serenaded constantly by a mix of bird song and cricket chatter, we entered Brienz. It had only taken us a couple of slow hours to get into the town and onto a lakeside campsite with neatly mown grass that was bathed in warm sunlight. After several nights of enduring constant cold, damp and even sub-zero temperatures this near Mediterranean campsite was one of the most welcome sites I could imagine.

As my human unpacked our sodden tent, I lay stretched out on the soft lawn. I was tethered to a small yew tree and stretched my tired body to its full length with a huge groan of contentment; heaven! The sun was brightly shining from across the lake. Its warmth heated my body and for the first time in almost a week, I felt both warm and dry. My sore feet and aching legs faded like a distant memory as I soaked up the warm rays.

Sadly we were allowed to stay just one night as the campsite was not dog friendly but as there were no other campers and I was so quiet, I was given a special dispensation. I was glad because there was no way I could have contemplated finding another location. I had set my heart on staying in this place and nothing was going to move me.

My human spread all of his kit out to dry and then joined me for an afternoon nap in the sun. As we snoozed the shimmering waves tumbled ashore breaking across the gravel bay with a soothing sound. Within a couple of hours, all of our kit was dry and we headed into town and an Italian restaurant for dinner.

We soon came up towards a small souvenir shop and stood outside was a bear! It stood eight feet tall and had its arms stretched upwards with its mouth open as the bear growled at passers-by. I lowered my stance and raised my hackles as high as they would go. I moved closer to the building line on my right and slowly crept forwards. I wanted to go far more slowly than my human would let me and could not work out until I got closer why he was not scared of the hungry bear. It was stuffed! I felt so stupid but had never seen a bear before.

I was feeling more like my normal self if not slightly embarrassed as we took our seat and a table on the terrace. As the afternoon turned to evening, a chill entered the air but it was still warm enough to eat outside and this would give me the chance to play with the waiting staff. I growled every time the waiter came out and nervously placed my humans' pizza on the table. I am certain that the waiter was glad to see us depart!

Despite the chilled evening air, we still returned to what was our warmest tent of the trip. The afternoon warmth still hung in the air within the tent as we settled down for a very quiet and at last a cosy nights sleep. The occasional passing trains merely seemed to add to the ambience of our location and soothed me to sleep. Outside of the tent the sky was clear and the silver moonlight bounced off the snow covered peak of the Faulhorn opposite.

On awaking the sky was still clear and a nice pale blue colour which promised our second day of good weather. The temperature had clearly risen and we could see the snow line receding upwards towards the mountain summits to the northern shore of the lake. This was the shore we would follow as we continued our westward journey.

The tent was quickly down and packed away. My humans pack would be significantly lighter today as only a small amount of morning dew hung on the fabric which previously had been soaked to the core in water and ice. We were very soon underway walking through town but we paused briefly at the local Co-op so that my human could stock up on some breakfast and lunchtime snacks.

My legs were very stiff and my feet were sore as we made our way into the forest above the lake. I was slow and looking forlorn which lead to a few sympathetic pats and strokes from a group of passing school children. I have managed to perfect the sorrowful look to the stage that people think my human is cruel for making me walk so far! Little do they know that I am only doing it in the hope of a bit of fuss and attention and hopefully some food! I once managed to look so pitiful as we walked from Oban to

Inverness that a waitress from a hotel barge which had moored in Fort Augustus gave me around half a pound of roast beef. She and my human chatted at length as I cleared the beef faster than the midges could bite me.

Unfortunately today no food was forthcoming. I quickly picked up my pace as soon as the last of the people had passed us.

The forest was dark and dense in places but regular clearings allowed us to benefit from the warm sun. My human was soon stripped down to his t-shirt which today, rather than being damp with Gore-Tex induced perspiration, was damp with sweat due to the warmth of the sun. Both of us were so used to being cold and damp that acclimatisation to the hot weather would be slow to achieve.

As we arrived at Oberried, my human spotted the local ferry coming into dock. He quickly clipped my lead on and we ran down the hill to the ferry terminal. This would be an unplanned boat trip that we would take so as to obtain full enjoyment of the Brienzer See.

The ferry was an old steamer freshly painted gleaming white in readiness for the summer season. Dogs are not allowed inside the steamers on Brienzer See so we went to sit on the foredeck. A small family group were our only company as I took up position on one of the slatted wooden seats. The varnished surface was both slippery and uncomfortable but did give me the opportunity to see over the sides of the boat and enjoy the panoramic view. It was stunning; an unbeatable mix of water, mountains, snow and sunlit blue sky. What more could a Smooth Fox Terrier want?

The ships horn sounded as we approached Iseltwald and I ducked as the sound vibrated through the seat and my body. I jumped off the seat in readiness to alight from the ferry but soon realised that we were to remain aboard. The picture postcard village grew ever nearer until we drew to a halt beside the pontoon. I watched as the crew jumped off the boat and then re-boarded at the last second as we pulled away from the pontoon. A young oriental couple had boarded the ferry and came to sit near me. I could tell that the girl was a little scared of me so I kept watching her and quietly growled in order to intimidate her. I enjoyed intimidating people and my human found it comical as he knew that I was well and truly restrained by my short lead but they did not!

A second brief stop at Bönigen heralded the final leg of our impromptu boat trip. The ferry turned to face Brienz and reversed along the Aare into Interlaken. We moored opposite the railway station, a place that was familiar to me as I had visited the veterinary surgeon in Interlaken the previous December during our Christmas trip to Lauterbrunnen. My human had also taken me into a store to buy me a new collar. He was unsure of my size so made me try the collar on. It was very embarrassing for me trying on new clothes in front of a female shop assistant. At least he did not remove my old collar or I would have had to stand in the middle of the store stark naked!

It was icy cold when we were last in Interlaken and the frozen ground was covered in snow. Happily today it was far warmer as we made our way towards the campsite beside the Aare. It was a tiny campsite and not very scenic but at least we would be near to local restaurants and shops to refresh ourselves prior to making our way to Lauterbrunnen in the morning. The ferry had given us a short day and a lazy afternoon beckoned; I would soon be fully refreshed and raring to continue my crossing of the Alps. Laying in the afternoon sun, I drifted in and out of a series of dreams. It was so relaxing and so nice to finally rest my tired paws.

The Valley of the Waterfalls

I WAS SURPRISED to wake up in a sunlit tent. Another nice day was most welcome but something I had become used to not seeing. Again my human would have a lighter pack as we walked up the valley to Lauterbrunnen. Part of me was sorry to say goodbye to Interlaken as our arrival there by boat had been so nice and relaxed but I was looking forward to heading up to more familiar ground and to seeing what the valley that had inspired Tolkien would look like without the frozen waterfalls that had adorned the valley walls during my last visit.

The walk to Lauterbrunnen was a gradual ascent through forest but accompanied constantly by a raging river with white water cascading over huge boulders, the winding road and the railway lines carrying trains whose coaches bulged with camera snapping Japanese people all clamouring to get the best views. Of course they were all on their way to Kleine Scheidegg and up through the Eiger to Jungfraujoch. This was a train journey I had done myself during the winter on a day when summit temperatures were below -19°C and my human and I actually had the summit to ourselves. On a day like today the mountain would probably feel like collapsing under the weight of trainer clad tourists who would rarely walk more than a hundred feet from the railway lines. I was glad that we were alone on the footpath.

Dappled sunlight broke through the overhanging branches and bird song gently filled the air over the roar of the passing river which was swollen with snow melt from the atrocious weather we had been enduring during the initial stages of our walk. The world was a different place with some sunshine and a light mist rose gently from the ground as its waterlogged surface warmed.

The scent of deer filled the air as we walked and squirrels darted back and forth leaping like oriental Olympic gymnasts from tree to tree. Unlike some dogs I do not bother chasing other creatures unless they are on the ground. Even then, if they are on my blind side, I normally fail to notice their presence.

Lauterbrunnen was reached all too soon and the comparative loneliness of the forest was breached by the hustle and bustle of the local railway station. The funicular up to Grütschalp was closed as it was being replaced by a cable car and huge tower cranes carried precarious loads overhead. Hoards of tourists were hurrying across the road to catch the bus service laid on to take the many thousands of fat lazy people, correction, the non-walkers up the Lauterbrunnental. It would be a nice ride for them but nowhere near as nice as it would be for me to walk it. It is only when one is on paw that the true experience of the surroundings can be obtained. The scent of meadow flowers, livestock, pine forest and the mountains would be filtered by the air conditioning systems of the coaches.

The narrow streets were overhung by timber chalets nestled between the steep valley sides which rose thousands of feet above us. Wengen looked down from our left whilst Murren stood proudly on the ridge to our right. The huge waterfalls cascaded thousands of tonnes of water down the rock face hitting their alluvial fans and spraying a thick mist over the surrounding vegetation. The huge plumes of water changed position with the wind.

We were to take up residence for a couple of nights in a campsite below one of those waterfalls. My human figured that two nights in Lauterbrunnen would not only offer an exploration opportunity but would also allow the fresh snow on the higher levels to melt thereby clearing the paths that would form the remainder of our route out of the German speaking regions and on into the French zones. I would soon change from being das hunde into le petite chein.

The campsite opposite Staubbachfall was nice; well laid out, quiet, clean and complete with an on-site restaurant and American girls on reception. They agreed to charge my humans' mobile phone which had gone flat a day or two earlier and also gave me lots of attention. I pushed my head against their hands and groaned with delight as they rubbed my ears; I exaggerated my enjoyment in order to wind my human up as I knew he would enjoy them doing it to him!

We were to have a lazy afternoon dozing in and out of sleep on the grass outside the tent. The last three days had all be relatively lazy and whilst I did feel a little guilty that we had missed walking over both Grosse Scheidegg and Kleine Scheidegg, I was comforted in the knowledge that I had walked both in full winter conditions only a few months earlier. At that time of year only serious walkers were on the routes but now both passes and in particular Kleine Scheidegg, would be amass with the sort of people my human and I strive to avoid; overweight, ice-cream eating tourists improperly dressed for the mountain in their sandals and high heels. Our previously peaceful walk through Wengernalp and Mettlenalp bore fond memories for me of blizzard conditions and the loneliness of white hillsides and alp buildings abandoned for the winter that we shared with no-one. To see them overrun by non-mountain folk would merely serve to tarnish those memories. Additionally, we would soon be crossing the Sefinenfurke via Rostock Hut and we would both need to summon all our stamina and maintain all our wits to cross this route successfully. A fall or injury on that route would have very serious consequences indeed and neither of us could afford any sort of mishap.

The next day was to be spent exploring the Lauterbrunnental. We had been here during the winter when we had stayed in a local chalet owned by on old lady with a blind dog called Meg that bumped into even more things than I ever do! We had left that chalet following a night of heavy snow and freezing rain. Conditions were treacherous on the roads until we reached Basel and even then caution was required all the way to Calais. However, it was now June and summer flowers adorned the flat valley floor in what was actually a graben; a faulted valley where the rock had collapsed downwards and been glaciated to produce a very impressive u-shaped valley.

I had a great time as we strolled along. I ran here, there and everywhere taking in every scent I could find and leaving a trail of my own on every prominent piece of ground or post. Large brown cows merrily rang their bells whilst their udders appeared full to bursting from their constant munching on the lush vegetation. My human was happy to have discarded his rucksack for a day and treated me to a tub of vanilla ice-cream. I licked and licked until the paper tub was almost worn through and sat with melted ice-cream smeared all over my long snout. Like a wayward four year old human, I had even managed to plaster the ice-cream across the top of my head and in my ears!

The soreness in my swollen pads had all but disappeared and the aching in my thighs and shoulders was fast becoming a distant memory. I lay stretched out in the bright, warm sunlight soaking up every bit of warmth I could find and ensuring I was fully recharged for our imminent departure. For us both, this was a well deserved day of rest following the trials of the previous week. From a distance perspective we were over half way but the route ahead was far more severe than anything that we had previously crossed. The passes would be higher and more remote and the quickly warming weather would lead to a far greater risk of blisters and dehydration. We had both endured similar before but not after such an arduous week. However, I was certain that we would make it; we had reached the halfway stage and were both far too determined to conquer the route to even contemplate turning back or catching the train to Sargans.

Prior to returning to the tent, we visited the Trümmelbachfälle, a huge waterfall which cascades down through tunnels it has carved through the base of the Silberhorn. We then stocked up on provisions for the next few days. We both ate heartily in order to stock up on enough carbohydrate to see us through the initial stages of tomorrows walk.

With work well underway to replace the local funicular, my human decided it best to set off up valley towards Stechelberg. Whilst this would avoid walking through Mürren with its picturesque streets and spectacular views of the Mönch, Jungfrau and Eiger, it would take us along the quieter and more remote paths through Sefinental.

The Schilthorn stood proudly above us stretching to its full height of 2,960m with the windows of the revolving Piz Gloria sparkling in the sunlight. Again I had been up there in the crisp still air of winter and enjoyed the 360° view of icy mountain peaks with their domes, pinnacles, spires, turrets, spikes and crags all encrusted with pure white snow and ice, whilst lesser humans stood in the warm inside watching clips from *On Her Majesty's Secret Service*, the film in which the restaurant had once featured.

Out of the trees and on into pasture, our path lead up to the Rostock Hut which had only just opened its doors to the public following its winter slumber. Our final ascent to the pass lay the other side of a basin of grass and rocks. The path crosses old moraines before a zigzag route crosses pad-destroying gritty black shale and scree one and a half hours after the hut. The summit of the pass made an ideal resting place where I re-gathered my thoughts in readiness for the descent which would be a tricky route down timber steps over shifting slopes of grit and scree protected with steel cables for my human to hold. The pass itself was very different to any I had seen previously being just a slight dip in a craggy ridge running north to south.

Although I was glad of the rest, I was growing increasingly nervous of the forthcoming descent. Drops all around us were steep and I knew that a slip would be the end of our walk if not the end of both of us. After a bite to eat and a cool drink, we set off. Remnants of snow adorned the path and provided an additional slippery hazard but also cooled my hot pads which had been heated by the friction of our gritty ascent. As my human attached my lead to my collar, I turned back for a last look at the Eiger, its Nordwand stood proud and I wondered whether any climbers were clinging to the 6,000ft face that had killed so many and I had stood both below and within earlier in the year. The spectacular view was what walking up the mountains was all about.

Carefully we descended with my human pausing occasionally to admire the tiny alpine plants adorning the walling rocks. In fact I think he was actually pausing to allow his knees to recover from the arduous descent but he would never admit to that! Each step required a slight jump from me which was followed by a skid on the loose surface; a skid that was only halted by the tension of my lead pulling against my neck. Each step hurt my feet and gradually each tug on my collar began to create an uncomfortable feeling in my throat. I stopped and coughed a few times but that did not really help.

Thankfully, after what seemed like a lifetime, we reached some grassy hillocks which meant an escape from my lead and some soft relief for my sore feet. The icy waters of a small stream provided me with light refreshment despite numbing my tongue and cheeks and accompanied us on a winding route down to Griesalp and our overnight accommodation at the local berghaus. They were expecting us a little earlier but a combination of the heat that we were still to acclimatise to and the steep descent from the pass, had delayed our entry into the tiny hamlet.

I looked around at the spectacular mountain scenery and knew that my human was thinking it would make an impressive base for exploring the local mountains. I hoped that such exploration would not be on the cards too soon and as I licked my feet, I wondered whether next year we may go mountain walking in the Netherlands with a geriatric rambling group. My human soon disturbed my day dream in order to take me upstairs to our room. It was a nice timber clad room with an en-suite bathroom and a large bed covered in crisp white linen; no chance of me sleeping on there though!

Hohtürli

THE PREVIOUS days eleven hour walk and steep descent had taken its toll on my shoulders but today I was told, would be shorter.; though I think it was actually me who was shorter! I hoped the day would be easier but my human also stated that today we would cross the Hohtürli, the highest pass on our route. I sighed in despair at the thought of a potentially tough climb.

My human had a large buffet style breakfast and managed to sneak out several slices of cheese, ham and sausage for me. I gulped it down far too quickly and had to cough some back up to re-chew. I knew I should not be so greedy but I also knew that I needed to eat whatever I was given in order to survive the day. The sight of meat and cheese was too much to bear and I could not possibly eat it all as fast as I wanted to.

My human knew that we could follow a road almost halfway to Hohtürli but he also knew that my feet were sore once again and decided that we should take a route through forest and pasture instead. I preferred this anyway as it meant that I could run free of my lead and stop to sniff for far longer before trotting to rejoin my human. Humans tend not to stop and sniff scents on the ground. I am not too sure why they do not do this as it is quite surprising what you can find. Sometimes I locate nice bitches that are on heat but up here, all I seemed to find were passing ewes and deer with the occasional marmot thrown in for good measure.

After crossing a few streams, we rejoined the road for a few minutes but this ultimately gave way to rough pasture and yet more of that slippery black grit. The grit was particularly slippery where it had been moistened by melting snow. No permanent path would ever survive the constant erosion. Runnels and gullies were everywhere on what turned out to be one of the severest slopes I have ever negotiated. Mind you, the severity did mean that height was gained with every step and upon reaching a rocky ridge the most amazing views were mine for the taking. There was so much to see that I longed to have my other eye back lest I miss some small detail.

Sadly, this was only the start of the worst bit! My human attached my lead to me again for what proved to be a steep traverse with long successions of splintering timber steps below overhanging crags. My human grazed his forehead a couple of times on the overhanging rocks which constantly fouled his heavy rucksack. With my lead in one had and the fixed cable in the other, my human trod carefully as we slowly made our way upwards. Ladders temporarily halted our progress as my human had to tie me at the bottom and ascend, leave his rucksack and descend to get me before proceeding to carry me up. I am not certain which was the more scary, the feeling of abandonment when he tied me at the base of each ladder and went ahead without me or being carried up a steel ladder with nothing but thin air below me. Heading up into the air with my feet off the ground was far from comfortable and my human did slip once or twice as the cool air had iced some of the rungs.

The metal rungs were worn smooth and silvery by the many pairs of boots that trod them yet the sides of the ladders were rusted and flaking. The old corroded bolts fastened to the rocks had stained the granite with dark brown streaks. I imagined that the ladders must have been many decades old and possibly formed part of the original via ferrata roots developed to carry troops over the mountains.

At last we reached the Hohtürli alive! The views were dominated by the Blümisalp massif and its receding glacier. The warming temperatures mean that all of the alpine glaciers are in recession and will soon disappear altogether. The beautiful masses of flowing ice have scoured the Alps for tens of thousands of years yet within just a few decades, human activity has reduced them to water and left bare, grey scars in their wake. You would not find any animals doing so much damage as the humans do. Mind you, my methane emissions may not help too much and there were certainly plenty of those on the steel ladders.

Kandersteg was next on our list and the way was well marked along a balcony overlooking glacial tongues whose ice was grey with rock and grit encased within it. Boulders and rocks littered the pastureland as we progressed through it and quickly grew closer to our days end.

Despite our route being along a well marked and well trodden path through pastureland, it was still hazardous. It seemed we had entered an area where all the cowpats in Switzerland had come to rest. Dry brown ones and wet green ones lay all around and try as I might to avoid them I inevitably ended up with it all over my paws! The culprits watched with big wide eyes as we passed them, their salivating tongues wrenching at the lush grass constantly fuelling their expulsion of excrement from the other end. All the way we were serenaded by constant bell ringing, mooing and splattering sounds as occasional goats bleated and ran away from us. All we needed now was Heidi but alas she was not to be found. My human stopped occasionally to talk to the cows as he stroked their heads but I was a little nervous of this as they were so much bigger than me and stupid enough to tread on my toes.

The glistening shoreline of Oeschinensee provided an escape from the cattle and an opportunity to wash my paws in the clear waters of the lake. Carved figures and animals adorned tree stumps along the shore and I made it my quest to ensure I cocked my leg against each and everyone one. This was easier said than done as both of my hind legs were too stiff to lift too high or too often. The signs for a chairlift also led the way to the campsite where we were to spend the night. Today had been an eventful and arduous one which had scared me at times and led to some interesting dreams as I slept in our tent.

Again dogs were not allowed on the campsite but my human negotiated that as long as I remained quiet and we left after just one night, we would be allowed to stay. I think the owners could see I was ready to drop so they agreed to my humans' proposal. The night was breezy but otherwise quiet and uneventful. Only two other tents had been erected on the site and the people with them seemed to be almost as tired me and my human.

Having managed to get ourselves up and moving in the morning, we proceeded through Kandersteg and past the International Scout Camp. I was still half asleep as we ascended a series of natural shelves through flower strewn meadows. Bees buzzed and crickets chattered all around me and I would occasionally snap at them if they came too close to my face. There would be no running around today, I was far too tired and had set my heart on just maintaining a steady pace behind my humans feet. Given half a chance I would have gladly laid among the flowers and dozed among the serenading crickets.

We were ascending to the Bunderchrinde, the last classic mountain pass of the APR which is nothing more than a tiny gap in a high ridge running from Gross Lohner to Allmegrat. The craggy ridge separates the Kandertal from Engstligental.

As we ascended, large grey clouds seemed to loom ever lower overhead. We were walking through steep woodland so it was difficult to see out and establish how good the visibility was but it was clear that the cloud was building. My human was slightly nervous about the clouds as the warm weather could lead to thunderstorms and of course, lightening. A thunderstorm in Glen Etive in Scotland had once pelted us with hail for almost an hour as it became trapped by the surrounding mountains. We had no choice but to seek shelter and avoid being struck by the many lightening bolts or hail stones. It was certainly a painful experience for both of us and lost us a considerable amount of time. Beyond the forest lay open scree slopes all the way to the pass and any crossing of the slope in a storm would be electrifyingly deadly.

Upon exiting the forest, my human decided that the clouds were just clouds and that no rain or storm would come though how he knew, I will never know. The gradient across the scree was comfortable though very exposed on the rough ground. Every step hurt as I made my way forward. The surrounding summits lurked eerily within the grey clouds as mountain merged into sky and vice versa. The narrow gap of the Bunderchinde was visible ahead as a thick drizzle began to soak my fur. This was the first rain for several days and was not at all welcome by either of us.

The drizzle soon subsided but left my coat feeling heavy and wet. The weather meant that we would not hang around on the pass but would descend without pausing. There was no view to be seen and the air was chilled and damp. Initially the descent was steep on loose ground with long zigzags leading across the grey screes. The cold breeze worked with the water in my coat to sap all the heat from my body. I shivered my way along the path with my teeth audibly chattering.

A small cattle byre provided shelter from the wind whilst we quickly ate. I longed for a scotch egg but all I was offered was a small amount of bread and some ham. Almost as soon as we had stopped, we were moving again; ever onward but thankfully downhill for the next couple of hours into the small town of Adelboden. I wished that the drizzle had held off for just a few hours longer as it would have allowed us to enjoy the view and relax in the sun. However, I know better than any dog that mountain weather is decidedly unpredictable and have spent many hours climbing to a summit just to sit and look at the inside of a cloud.

The campsite at Adelboden was on a scrap of land squeezed into the edge of town. No other tents were on the site and I am not sure any more could have fitted. Several caravans were occupied but we appeared to be attracting a lot of interest because we had appeared on foot looking tired and damp. The weather had suddenly turned extremely cold and damp but had resulted in good progress being made in an effort to keep warm and before dusk my human and I headed into town and enjoyed a well earned meal at a local restaurant.

The staff were dog friendly and I was given some left over pizza. The spices on it made me sneeze but it was good to get some food that warmed me up and as we ate, the cloud quickly began to clear. I walked back to the tent with a bulging stomach and was already falling off to sleep as I curled myself into a tight ball at the foot of my humans' sleeping bag. Even the headlights and noise of cars passing on the road above failed to disturb my sleep.

Warmer Weather

I AWOKE TO the gentle warmth of the rising sun which softly illuminated the inside of our tent. My limbs were stiff and aching as I stretched and yawned before rolling onto my back. I had ensured that my wriggling was enough to wake my human thus ensuring that my chest and belly would be tickled as I lay quivering lightly.

My human was in no hurry to get up and took advantage of the sun's warmth to dry the morning dew from the tent as we both relaxed. Breakfast took the form of a couple of pain au chocolat that we had purchased the previous night. My human ate the bulk of them and I was fed a couple of small scraps. I choked slightly as I chewed them because I had been too lazy to roll from the prone position I had adopted with my legs in the air. The slight choking increased to a somewhat threatening cough so my human lifted me and rotated me onto my feet before proceeding to pat me on my back. The pastry came back up into my mouth and I proceeded to chew it and swallow; no chance of my human stealing food from my mouth!

We got out of the tent and headed out for a walk so that I could cock my leg a few times. The grass on the campsite was long but as we walked towards the toilet block, the roar of a sit-on lawnmower drowned the sound of morning birdsong. As my human tied me to a bench outside the toilets, I watched the site owner circle the caravans. The blades of the lawnmower easily chopped through the long damp grass which filled the air with its scent.

My human was having his first shave in days. Often on long walks he would go for four or five days without shaving. I think it was partly through laziness but also because he always carried a cheap plastic razor with him on long walks as they are lighter than his usual metal one. As soon as his whiskers began to approach the length of mine, he would shave.

The sound of the owners' lawnmower mesmerised me as I watched it trundle back and forth over and over the same bits of grass time and again. As I sat waiting my mind began to wander. I wondered what I would look like if I shaved my face like my human does. Would I look suave and sophisticated or would I look a bit of a prat. I remember the old man once shaving his white beard off and he looked like Wilfred Bramble; the dirty old man! Mind you, my skin would not be so worn and wrinkled so I may look ok kind of like a canine Brad Pitt. Mmm......I thought that maybe I should sneak into the bathroom when we got home. I would have to be careful not to get shaving foam everywhere and would struggle to reach the mirror but I was sure I could manage it. I could imagine the surprised look on my humans face if he was to return from work and find me shaven! I have heard of beavers shaving but never a dog.

It seemed like an age had passed before my human reappeared. He smelt far better and looked more human; far tidier. Back at the tent, he had a quick drink and then proceeded to take the tent down. The fabric was nice and dry and was taught across the pole. It seemed such a shame to be leaving the tranquillity of the campsite. With the sun shining brightly I was very sad to be saying goodbye to the elderly people who sat staring from their steamy caravan windows. Every move we made was observed and commented upon. I felt like a goldfish but knew they were still somewhat bemused as to what we were doing on foot. To be honest, I could not really blame them as it was a thought that had been ever present in my mind since we had started up the hill out of

Sargans. I was still unsure how far we were going but my human kept saying we were nearly there so I knew the end was nigh.

With the tent down and packed tightly into its bag within just three or four minutes, we were ready to go. My human swung his pack onto his bag and attached my lead to his hip belt. We strode purposefully out of the campsite. Well my human strode purposefully whilst I kind of limped and snuffled my way out. My legs felt very stiff and sore and my feet were tender but I was as fit as I would ever be so I soldiered on.

Almost at a march we crossed and re-crossed the river as we walked upstream out of the centre of Adelboden. A couple of people said "Bonjour" as we passed them. My human responded with the same though each time he hesitated as after days of exchanging German greetings he struggled to get to grips with being in a French speaking region. It was easier for me, a woof is a woof wherever you are although the accents are slightly different and French bitches smell nicer than their English or German counterparts, particularly those poodles. Ouch! As my mind wandered onto the poodles, I stopped concentrating and walked straight into a fence post on my blind side! It was not the first time and certainly would not be the last. Thankfully I have a solid head and barely notice the dull thud as I wander into things. My human reckons it is a case of no sense, no feeling. I am not too sure why he says that as I am quite an intellectual dog but I guess he is just a dumb human and knows no better.

Soon we were alongside a small woodland and I was finally allowed off my lead. This was the perfect opportunity for me to concentrate on sniffing as opposed to making progress. I was tired and did not really want to be walking. I was doing it under protest today as I would have been quite happy to vegetate outside the tent for the day but that was not to be.

The scent of marmot and deer was strong on the ground. The lush long grass beside the woodland was damp from the previous days mist and drizzle. The sun was quickly drying the vegetation it touched but the trees of the woodland provided shade from its warmth and the dampness retained the aroma of every passing animal. It would be a bloodhound's idea of heaven but my nostrils were not so sensitive. Plumes of steam rose silently from the leaves and grasses that were exposed to the warmth of the sun.

Suddenly the grass moved. There was something in there, something alive and moving. I wondered what it was and jumped lunging heavily down on the moving grass in an effort to grab the creature in my paws as I bore down on it with silently opened jaws. Yikes! Just my luck, the beast I had captured was a hedgehog. Its prickles stuck into my face and paws; I was impaled. Quickly I backed off and barked in the hedgehogs face. A deep and meaningful bark designed to shock it into staying still. The hedgehog rolled itself into a flea-infested ball which I proceeded to tap with my paws as I barked and moaned playfully at it.

My human turned and walked back to where I was barking. He wanted to see what I had captured. "Look!" I said, "I have captured a vicious and threatening killer hedgehog". I was proud of my bravery and eagerly wagged my tail and panted with excitement as I awaited the undoubted praise I would receive for saving my human from being slain by a blood thirsty hedgehog. But he was not impressed. Did he not realise my bravery? Obviously not. "Leave it alone" he commanded. Of course I ignored him for I knew that if I took my eye off this creature for just one second, it may launch an attack. "Harry!" he exclaimed gruffly, "leave it".

My human was not happy. He grabbed my collar and tugged me away from the prickly predator. I had been half slung in the direction we were to walk. Unimpressed at my bravery, my human ensured that I stayed ahead of him for a while until we were well

away from the hedgehog. I guess that my prey would have un-
furled itself and proceeded on its way, collecting slugs and bugs
for its breakfast as it waddled through the undergrowth. I vowed
never to risk my life like that for my human again, well least not
until the next time.

The temperature was rising rapidly and had already surpassed the
warmest temperatures we had so far experienced. This would create another problem; gone was the risk of frostbite, now it would
be dehydration and heat stroke. As the sun rose higher overhead,
my panting started in earnest. The patches of snow that lay round
about were rapidly thawing as we climbed higher and higher towards the saddle of Hahnenmoospass.

Before the pass was reached we entered Geils, a small cluster of
buildings at 1,707m which upon our arrival were all but deserted.
With the ski season over and done with, only a small team of
maintenance staff remained. To the sound of hammering ema-
nating from a bearded chap who was sitting astride the ridge of a
nearby rooftop, I wandered over to a water trough and began lapping at the cool water that was pouring into it.

The sky was a deep blue and sparkling waterfalls adorned the surrounding hills. An elderly black dog half walked and half stag-
gered over to me. We sniffed and exchanged a few words. The dog
was called Henri and his walking days were long since over. The
poor chap could barely rise to his feet and collapsed in a heap as
soon as he had finished saying hello to me. I had a feeling that
when Henri was younger, he would have guarded the trough and
fought any unfamiliar dogs in order to protect the supply. Yet now
he was just a little grumpy and resigned to watching through fail-
ing eyes. I politely thanked Henri as my human patted him and
we made our way out of Geils towards the summit of the pass. I
was glad I had not been forced to fight the old dog, it would have
been a shame to hurt him.

I looked back a couple of times and saw that Henri was watching us fade into the distance. I knew he wanted to follow and was missing the joys of running across the mountains. I hoped I would never grow old and have to watch my human fade into the distance across the mountains. I am not getting any younger but there is still plenty of life in me. However, I know I am not immortal and the thought of not being able to remain active terrifies me.

Our minor tarmac road rose easily from the buildings and within forty-five minutes we were at the pass. The pass is very accessible and can apparently be very busy as a result but upon our arrival the hotel was empty and we had the mountain to ourselves. My human paused for a time to eat some chocolate before we began our descent which gently eased along the hillside to Büelberg.

Eerily this village was also empty as though abandoned due to some strange happenings. I wandered up onto the balcony of a nearby chalet and peered down at my human as he passed below. He half watched me in case I decided to jump from the balcony. He need not have worried, the day was good and I was content. Now had I found a similar balcony as we crossed Foo Pass, the story may have been somewhat different!

I trotted down the blackened timber steps and ran to catch up with my human. The weather had lifted me despite the sudden extreme heat and I was happy to be out and about.

A signed path led down to Lenk which I could see laying in the valley below. The Simmental was flowing to our right and its sparkling waters tempted me. Suddenly something moving on the hillside caught my attention. My human noticed it as I did and he quickly grabbed hold of my collar. The animal smelt like a cat but was far bigger than any tabby I had ever seen. It was a huge wildcat and had already sensed our presence. My human clipped my lead to my collar and fumbled to get his camera from the ruck-sack. The big cat was too canny for us though and quickly slipped into the shadow of some nearby trees and seemed to melt into the undergrowth. We both stood watching motionless hoping that the big cat would re-appear but sadly it was not to be. The cat had made good its escape from our gaze but left us both with a lasting memory of its sight.

After a few minutes spent waiting for the cat to show itself again we gave up and continued our journey through the houses at Brandegg, a sprawling farming community. Pretty dark timber chalets dotted the hillside and lush meadow grass swayed gently all around us with colourful flower heads dancing among the brown blades of grass. The wind gently whooshed through the fields as we reached the town that marked the end of the railway line through the Simmental.

Lenk is a tiny old spa town built on flat ground within what was a marshy section of the Simmental. We made our way to the campsite at the far end of the village and my human erected the tent. This was the first time since our initial arrival in Liechtenstein that a dry tent had been erected. Again we had the only tent on the site and just a handful of caravans were occupied.

We both dozed for an hour or so before making our way back into the town for some dinner. When we had first passed through, the town was empty but now it was full of scouts and guides. Uniformed juveniles were everywhere but all were polite and well behaved and, I am glad to say, all of them wanted to say hello to "le petite chien". I was in my element!

One bowl of pasta later and we were on our way back to the tent. It was still early and the sun was still warm as we both lay in the tent with the doors open. The breeze gently blew through the tent. The rustling of the fabric soothed me as I lay dreaming. As the sun dropped below the mountain tops, the temperature began to fall. Before darkness had arrived, my human secured the tent and drifted off to sleep. My slumber soon followed and I would remain in a deep sleep for the next twelve hours.

Hotel Bären

WE WERE having a good run on the weather. When we awoke the sun was shining brightly and the tent was bone dry again. My human liked a dry tent as it would be lighter to carry. The tent was quickly down and we were soon on our way to the local bakery. My human had eaten all of his food and needed to restock for the day.

The bakery was at the far end of town but was on our route so I was happy to stop by. The window of the bakers was adorned with marzipan ladybirds and bees. My mouth watered as I gazed longingly at the food on display but I would not be treated to anything. The rich aroma of freshly baked bread wafted from the doorway and across my acutely sensitive nostrils, I can almost eat the smell which was making my mouth water profusely. We sat outside for a time as my human drank half a litre of milk and then we departed. I was sad to leave the bakers shop. With no scouts or guides in sight, Lenk was once again a quiet and idyllic Swiss town.

The day ahead was to be a long one so my human decided we would take the Betelberg Gondola in order to get up to the top of the first pass before the temperature rose too high. The view from the gondola as we shook and vibrated our way upwards was amazing. I was able to look down on a small herd of deer and they had no idea I was watching. How I longed to pounce down on them like a wolf. Fortunately for them, I was contained in a metal box with Perspex windows.

The ground below the gondola was very rough in places and I could see a roadway snaking its way up the hillside. I was glad to be riding through the sky without having to endure the pounding that my feet would undoubtedly have taken. Though I must admit that the thought of the few poorly lubricated wheels and thin cable holding us did make my stomach somersault occasionally particularly when we passed the pylons and which momentarily vibrated and swung the carriage.

All too soon we reached the top and had to get out of the gondola. The man operating it appeared surprised to see us getting off as all the other cars were empty. We were aiming for the Stüblenepass and down into Lauenen. The hillside was deserted as we continued onwards and upwards. A couple of chamois darted ahead of us. I was half tempted to follow but whilst my mind was prepared for the chase my legs were not. I was tired and sore so decided it far safer to stay near to my human. At least that way I could look alert without suffering the embarrassment of my pursuit turning into a lethargic hobble.

I was tired and my mind was wandering. I failed to notice that at a fork in the path my human turned left whilst I continued to the right. I had gone a few hundred yards before I realised the error of my ways and by this time my human was out of site. As I was walking behind him, he failed to notice that I had taken a wrong turn and had carried on walking at a brisk pace.

I started to panic and ran aimlessly around looking for him but to no avail. There was no option but to re-trace my steps but when I got back to the junction, there was still no sign. However, by now he had noticed I was missing and I could hear him calling my name. Trouble was, with the echo from the surrounding mountains and the roar of the wind, each shout was echoed several times and I had no idea where the initial shout was coming from.

I searched high and low and then as quickly as he had vanished, he re-appeared. I was so pleased and excited to see him that I ran over and leapt at him like a puppy. "You stupid human" I thought, "You almost got yourself lost!" Of course, I knew it was really me who had made the mistake but silently blaming my human made me feel so much better.

A single strand of rusting barbed wire ran along the broad ridge with the pass itself over to our left. We made our way across to the pass on a well trodden and wide path. Two other hikers were now following behind but at the fence they turned right and headed for Trüttlisberg Pass. I ducked under the wire as my human stepped over the top. The wire looked as though it had been there from the Second World War, its rotting posts leant away from the prevailing wind and dead grass clung helplessly to the many corroded spikes.

Descending steeply at first we started on a series of long loops towards Lauenen. Boulders were dotted all around us and two old people were walking towards the top that we had just left. She was very old and wrinkled and looked about ninety and he looked almost twice her age. Their leathery and wrinkled faces were darkly tanned from the alpine sun and their brows were glistening with sweat. Both said bonjour and smiled broad toothless smiles as they passed by and both commented on me though neither I nor my human had a clue what they were saying. They were a nice old couple but both needed a good scrub and a change of clothing. I guess in their way they were happy and walking up such a steep hill was a credit to their health and determination.

It was lunchtime when we arrived in Lauenen and the shop was closed. There was however a hotel nearby with several picnic tables in the garden. My human decided to stop for a proper meal rather than continue walking on a snack. He tied me to a table and went inside to obtain a menu. Several wealthy looking couples were sitting nearby and all seemed somewhat put out that a sweaty hiker and his dog had invaded their idyllic garden. We were doing no harm though; I was tied to my humans' pack which he had laid near to the furthest table. I was not even showing any interest towards the ducks that were cockily wandering around in front of me quacking their annoyance at my presence. At least the ducks spoke their minds unlike the snobbish people. They should have been pleased to have such a handsome dog patronising their local hotel. After all, I had taken the time to walk the length of their country to eat with them when all they had done was extract their fat rears from the leather clad seats of their gas guzzling cars.

My human soon came back outside with a menu and was watched intently by the others as he strode across the lawn. Every move he or I made was watched and commented upon but none more so that my growling at the plump old waitress when she came to take the order. My human ordered schnitzel and proceeded to check the map as the waitress waddled back across the lawn like the overfed ducks.

Within a few minutes the waitress returned with my humans' food. He took a firm hold of my nose so that I could not lunge at her as she placed the food on the table and then he proceeded to eat under the gaze of the onlookers. None of them stopped for long though and we soon had the sun drenched garden to ourselves. We sat in dappled shade with the warm sun filtering comfortingly through the leaves of overhanging trees. As we sat watching the ducks and listening to the buzzing of the bumble bees, it seemed far too nice a place to leave but we had no choice but to push on. We had a second pass to cross before Gsteig and our next campsite could be reached.

We walked from the garden just as an E Type Jaguar sped by; its six cylinder engine screaming up through the gears. I jumped as the vibration of the Jaguar vibrated through my feet. I longed to be sitting in the front seat with the cool air ruffling my fur and flapping my ears but alas I just had the reflected heat of the sun drenched tarmac cooking my underbelly as I soldiered on along the narrow road. Ahead the Wildhorn stood proudly with an outstretched snowy mantle above a hanging valley beckoning us on. A signpost pointed to the right to the Krinnen Pass and Gsteig. We crossed the babbling Louibach and proceeded up a winding farm road past a handful of run down farmhouses. A scruffy Lhasa Apso barked wildly as we passed by its garden. I silently cocked my leg against the garden fence part in disgust at the other dog's behaviour but also to stamp my authority upon the scruffy mutt.

We were soon into boggy meadows and squelching uphill away from the track and on into trees that led up to Sattel. The path became even wetter as we climbed through dense woodland and passed an elderly couple and their tiny granddaughter. The toddler smiled and greeted me with a squeal. She stroked me vigorously which felt great. I like little people; my human has a friend called Shirley who looks after me sometimes if he has to work late and cannot take me with him. She is only little and so are her children. I think they may be a Hobbit family but am not certain. When I stretch to my full height, I can almost look them directly in the eye.

The little girl seemed to gain momentum after stroking me and scrambled up the hill after me without giving a second thought to the mud and undergrowth which had previously hampered her progress. Soon we were stood in a gap on the wooded ridge, this was the Krinnen Pass. Ahead lay the limestone massif of Les Diablerets, Col du Pillon and the Saanental. My human and I awaited the arrival of the girls grandparents before making our way out of the woodland and down into the valley. They looked fit to drop by the time the pass was reached and barely had the energy to restrain their granddaughter as we left them all behind.

The little girl was crying as she wanted to chase "le petit chien" but I was in no mood to be chased any longer. I needed my bed!

A twisting road with a narrow gravel path following a straight route through the zigzags took us down to Gsteig. This was a pretty village built in a lineal style along a single main road. Several horses grazed quietly in fields behind the houses as crops matured in the sun. We turned left onto the road and walked through the town and out to the campsite. Or so we thought. Where the campsite should have been, a building site now existed. The campsite had apparently closed at the end of last season and was now being covered in timber chalets. We had nowhere to sleep!

With no other campsite in town and wild camping being banned in Switzerland, there was no option but to head back down the hill into town. Three hotels exist in the tiny town but one was being refurbished and a second was closed. Thankfully, as luck would have it, the nicest hotel was open and had rooms available. The amazingly pretty Hotel Bären which was built in 1756 has fantastically decorated gables and is staffed by friendly Portuguese girls.

My human explained our predicament and we were presented with a double room overlooking a stream which cascaded noisily below the window. The receptionist was friendly and helpful and the room spotlessly clean. The hotel stop was unexpected but very welcome to a very tired dog and a human who was in need of a shower. My human spent what seemed like hours in the shower taking full advantage of the cleanliness and warmth of the hotel after almost two weeks of showering in cold and at times dirty shower blocks. As for me, I managed to sneak up on the bed whilst he was showering and buried myself in the soft down filled duvet. It was doggy heaven and whilst I was expecting to be slung off the bed after he had showered, to my surprise I was allowed to stay up there. My human lay beside me on the bed and we both drifted off to sleep.

Sleep and home comforts put aside any thoughts of food and we both slept soundly until the morning. We were up early and soon headed down stairs so that my human could eat some breakfast. The same girl who had shown us to our room was serving break-fast and seemed pleased to see us. A table had been set near to the window with a buffet selection of bread, meats and cheese laid out on another table nearby.

I watched as my human filled his plate with enough food to feed a family of four for a week! He ate and ate until he must have been ready to explode and without giving me a morsel he said his goodbyes and we left the hotel.

Journey's End

WE HAD only been walking for about five minutes when my human decided to sit down on a bench. At first I thought he had eaten too much but I was soon being given sliced meat and cheese that he smuggled out of the hotel. It was great to taste something other than biscuits. Like my human, I ate heartily before we set off once more towards Col des Mosses.

The walk out of Gsteig was a steep ascent up wooded hills. Rabbits scurried across the path as we puffed and panted our way toward the edge of the woodland and a farm building. Cows stood gazing idly at us as we passed by. Their mouths were slowly chewing at the grass as their bells rang out across the hillside. The smell of their dung was hidden amidst the sweet smell of pine needles and the aroma of wild garlic. However, the aroma of rotting manure burned at my nostrils as we neared the farm buildings.

A moist brown carpet lay underfoot making me wonder at what the farmer was feeding his cows on! Just before we reached the farm buildings, a path on the left took us up a steep meadow and on into a dense forest of wild raspberries. Here my human ate as we walked, tearing off handfuls of succulent raspberries as we progressed across the meadow. The grass was long and filled with stunning wild flowers of every colour. I ploughed my way through it and came out the other side with my head coated in a mix of pollen and cuckoo spit.

The raspberries gave way to a grove of fir trees with views of Les Diablerets tempting us to continue moving forward. More pastures had to be crossed and all were steep until finally we reached the saddle of the Blattipass at 1,900m. The grassy shrub-covered ridge has the most memorable eastward view of all the passes on the Alpine Pass Route. My human sat against one of the trees that dotted the crest of the pass and gazed back at the complete line of the Bernese Oberland. The sun was high and the day was clear, the Wetterhorn, Eiger and waves of snowy summits stretched all the way to the slabs of Les Diablerets and its glacial tongues.

As my human sat and absorbed the view, I rolled contentedly in the lush grass. My legs were flailing in the air and I groaned in delight as I soaked up the warmth of the sun. Then I started to roll down the hill and had to quickly stop myself and struggle to my feet. I walked up towards my human with both my ears turned inside out. My human flicked them back around the right way for me and sat stroking me for a few minutes before we began our descent over grassy slopes and through small clumps of trees.

Col des Andérets came quickly and was a chance for me to look back for the last time at the Oberland peaks. The Eiger could still be seen standing proudly among the glistening white summits. I had enjoyed walking among those mountains but my sore feet and aching limbs bore testament to the physical demands they had placed upon my aging canine bones. The Arnensee glistened temptingly below, its waves shimmering silver in the sunlight. However, on the other side of the col, the Dents du Midi beckoned us forward. Montreux and Lake Geneva were drawing ever closer.

As we descended towards Isenau, my heart began to sink. The walking so far had been arduous and at times, we were lucky to be able to continue walking but Montreux was to be the end of our journey and I was not sure I wanted it to end. Returning to the mundane routine of life in England, whilst not such a bad life, really did not appeal. I had honed my mountain skills over the past two weeks and I knew that the mountains were my true home far away from the hustle and bustle of an urban life in England.

At Restaurant D'Isenau, we stopped for lunch. The restaurant itself was closed but there was seating nearby and shelter from the hot sun. We sat enjoying a mixture of cheese and sausage before continuing to Meitreile where a scenic belvedere path kept us high above the valley. It was a truly spectacular panorama and I could imagine that the cows grazing below us were totally relaxed in their surroundings.

A group of dark timber alp buildings at La Dix welcomed us and provided my human with the opportunity to purchase some cold fresh milk. We shared a litre before progressing towards Col Des Mosses. Mont Blanc stood to the left of Dents du Midi and was clearly the highest point around. Memories of my previous walk on the Tour du Mont Blanc came flooding back. That had been my first long distance foreign walk and another extremely memorable experience. Walking from Switzerland through Italy and on into France before returning to our start point in the small Swiss resort of Champex. My feet had been sore at the end of that walk too!

Col Des Mosses was reached and not a moment too soon. The heat had taken its toll on both of us and I was panting hard. The cool water of the village fountain provided welcomed refreshment to us both and a chance to gather our bearings before heading to our penultimate campsite just outside of town. My human took the liberty of standing me in the fountain whilst I drank my fill of the icy waters. Every part of my underside was well and truly soaked and cooled.

It was to be a warm and sticky night in the tent which was bad news for the long day ahead. The snow-capped mountains that had accompanied us for so long were now left far behind but the scenery was still something special. Deeply carved valleys with steep forested walls rising to bleached ribs of limestone abounded with rowan and beech providing much needed but infrequent shade as we continued towards our final pass at Col de Chaude.

The heat was taking its toll on both of us as we finally left the hot tarmac surface of the road that had led us along the shores of Lac de l'Hongrin. Water fowl chatted noisily as we passed them all seemingly worried by my presence as they swam and waded in the sparkling water where they competed with colourful sailboards.

At the end of the lake we entered a cool tunnel. Its damp musty air giving stark relief from the heat of the sun outside to the extent that it almost took my breath away. The light at the end of the tunnel shone dazzlingly into my eye causing me to blink and occasionally wander into my humans legs. The heat outside could be felt before we had even reached the tunnels mouth and the bright sunshine burnt the black tip of my nose as we exited into the steeply walled Hongrin.

As we descended, lizards of all shapes and sizes darted back and forth across our path. Initially I was curious about them but they were far too energetic and impossible to catch so I soon gave up chasing them and decided instead to concentrate my energies into a steady plod behind my human. His tall body gave some shade from the midday sun as I panted down the rough and dusty path.

Occasional streams gave welcomed relief from the dusty conditions serving to both quench my thirst and wash the limestone grit from my tongue. A thin crust of dust lined my nostrils to which it stuck as the breeze whipped it up into mini-tornado like swirls from the ground. Crickets chattered endlessly as I brushed through the long brown grass that lined our pathway. The flowers that had once adorned the path were now brown and dehydrated, baked stiffly by the relentless heat.

At Col de Chaude we both sat down and enjoyed our first glimpse of Lake Geneva. Over the years we had travelled past the clear waters of the lake many times in the car but from here it looked more magical than ever. It was the end of our journey and this first sight of our journeys end saw the lake gleaming brightly in the sun as a steamer paddled its way towards Evian. The mountains of France stood on the far bank as fading profiles in the heat haze. From now on it would be downhill all the way. But the paths were steep, dusty and narrow. Thankfully they were also heavily wooded by tinder dry trees and shrubs which provided some shade for me on the descent.

In the clearings soft grass gave welcome relief to my feet whilst craggy rocks provided ample opportunity for leaving my scent without the need to stray too far from my human. We took our final rural refreshments at Auberge de Sonchaux before entering Glion and choosing to take the Funicular into Montreux rather than descend thousands of concrete steps to the lake shore 45 minutes walk below.

The old funicular carriage clattered and clunked its way down hill through the hustle and bustle of the noted resort that has plied its trade for more than 200 years. I was certain that the funicular was also 200 years old and feared for my safety as we appeared to be descending on a loose track! Rickety as the carriage was, we were soon standing within the confines of the main railway station in Montreux and within minutes were standing on the shore of lake.

Our final destination would be a lakeside campsite at Vevey which sits away from the surfeit of high-rise hotel blocks just half an hour along the lake shore. My legs had stiffened on the funicular and as I limped my way through the gardens and across the beaches on the lakeshore, I gained endless sympathetic pats and compliments from the plethora of young topless female sunbathers whose athletic golden tanned bodies adorned the lakeside. Some were so enthusiastic with their attention that I feared I may lose my remaining eye! It was just reward for a small one-eyed Fox Terrier at the end of a two hundred and fifty mile walkies.

ISBN 142517865-0

25227630R00074

Printed in Great Britain
by Amazon